# My Odyssey With Two Uncommon Boys:

## A Trip To The Western States

Ethel Erickson Radmer

My Odyssey With Two Uncommon Boys:
A Trip To The Western States

Book Cover Design by Tammy Radmer

Published by Euphonia Publishing, North Carolina
euphoniapublishing@gmail.com
Printed in the USA


ISBN 978-0-9651182-2-4


The author thanks the two young men in the book for their
invitation to me to join them on the trip to the Western States
and for their editing of my book
Thanks also to Tammy Radmer, Editor and Cover Artist extraordinaire

# FOREWORD

This is a true story. I have only changed the names of the two boys who are the main characters. Some conversations I have written exactly as they were spoken while others I have changed somewhat or reconstructed. But they all reflect the truth of who and what the boys are. Everything is in their voice, their spirit, their knowledge, and their character. Both boys have approved all the conversations as I have written them, as well as my descriptions of our escapades together. Their actions are theirs, encoded with their unique thinking processes. To the best of my ability, I have been true to their nature and their projection onto and response to life.

Both boys have had diagnostic labels suggested in their early years, to be questioned and either accepted, altered, or discarded later. As the boys' behaviors have become more "normal," i.e. more acceptable to the general public, professionals have adjusted their list of "disorders."

Today, with the sharp increase in autism-related diagnoses and theories of possible causes, behavioral scientists are unable to point to any one cause. And they have had to increase their list of possible diagnoses or labels, and increase the breadth of possible exhibited behavior within each label.

What I call "sensory disorders" and I would describe as "the brain taking in information from and for the senses in an unusual way," is a broad continuum of overlapping disorders encompassing

ADD, ADHD, Asperger's Syndrome, Autism, Dyslexia, Dyspraxia, Obsessive Compulsive Disorder, Savant Syndrome, Sensory Integration Dysfunction, Synesthesia and Tourette's Syndrome.

These labels can be helpful, but can also mask the truth. The truth of these boys is beyond labels, so in the main text, I have chosen not to use diagnostic labels that describe behavior. I only show how the boys acted, how they communicated and how they talked. I do not want the reader to see their behavior through the prism of a label. I believe that labels would limit the readers' understanding, and narrow their experience of what is a rainbow spectrum of human expression. Not using labels also frees us to appreciate the beauty and brilliance of these two boys. And freedom is what these boys most want – freedom from criticism and not fitting in. Our humanity calls for us not to set apart or shut out another human being with a tease or a rejection, a rebut or a denial. We all wish for acceptance. With an open heart we can feel the awe of the incredible variations of our being.

This book is about a trip that these remarkable boys and I made together to explore part of America and to get a better idea of the Nation's history. History is part of all humanity. In our travels, we learned more about who we are.

The boys are uncommon in their interests, their perceptions and their actions. They have unusual and unique qualities and aspirations. We all have someone in our lives (maybe even ourselves) who seems set apart from the mainstream of humanity. We should celebrate our individuality. We are all uncommon in our own way. We give homage to our creation, to our diversity, and to the beauty that nature manifests in us and around us.

# CONTENTS

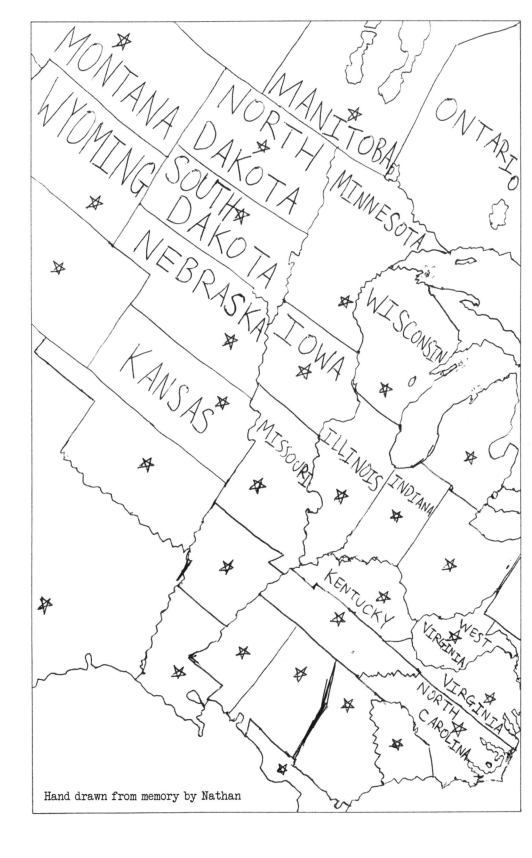

Hand drawn from memory by Nathan

# Before They Met

Two boys are sitting in a sand box. Almost four years old, they are. Beauteous good looks. Quiet as the air. Intent on what they are doing. They play side by side, but each is alone. They seem not to notice the other, yet they could touch if they stretched out their arms. One boy is lining up his plastic, sand cups. All in a row, on the sand, are the yellow ones. The green ones are in a separate line, the shortest first, then on up to the tallest. A faint smile shows on his lips. Satisfaction with what he sees.

His neighbor has plastic blocks. He smoothes out a flat place in the sand with his delicate hands and he stacks the multicolored cubes in a tower. High up it goes. He seems to know precisely how to position them so that they don't tip and he looks with glee at his engineering marvel.

They share a focus, these blond boys with cherubic faces. An attention to groupings of size and color, an intent to line up or stack. Categorizing, systematizing. An ordered world they have made for themselves. But they are in separate worlds.

Neither one speaks. The boy with blocks does glance toward the rows of cups and then back to his tower. He looks in awe as it tips and tumbles softly into the sand. The row maker, oblivious to the fall of blocks, stays intent on his cups, lining up a new orange row, a match for his orange shirt. He favors orange.

# CHAPTER 1

# INVITATION

Nathan and Kenny met each other in their freshman year of high school. But, they both lived in the same North Carolina capital city area from the time that they were born. Possibly playing in the same playgrounds and sitting in the same sandboxes without knowing it. Both were alone in their own worlds.

In their separate elementary schools, they continued to be alone. Then slowly, through the years, they ventured into the society of their classmates, first looking and listening, then maybe bravely conversing with a few. In ninth grade, Nathan was a little more social than Kenny but still not mixing with others. By eleventh grade Nathan was almost as social as most of the other high school students, with Kenny still behind.

Nathan and Kenny first noticed each other in the halls, just saying hi to each other's receptive face. They had literature and biology classes together and then became lab partners, which can be a cauldron for a budding friendship. Nathan thought that Kenny was a soccer-playing jock and did not see him as a potential friend. But, they seemed to sense something in the other that was a little different from most of the other kids. Maybe it was their quiet way of being or their not quite getting all the social and classroom rules. After a class trip, when they were roommates, their friendship grew. Throughout the rest of high school, they were pals and had an assortment of other friends. After graduation, Nathan went on to a college in Wisconsin. Kenny enrolled in North Carolina State.

In February of 2005, during their freshman year at their respective colleges, Nathan, who is my grandson, called me on the phone from his dorm in Wisconsin.

"Kenny and I have an idea," he excitedly told me. "We want to make a car trip through the Western States." And then he sweetly, but firmly offered, "We both want you to go with us. Will you come?"

Now, I've known these boys a long time. I met Kenny when he and Nathan first became friends. He always was a quiet, sweet boy, and now is a smart, polite young man. He surprises with a sly, ingenious turn-of-mind. Nathan, I have known since my daughter gave him birth. I have seen a babe filled with secrets, slowly reveal a brilliance of mind. Like a butterfly, hidden in a chrysalis emerging into an imago of color. Nathan, Kenny and I have done a lot of things together – playing word games that we make up, going to the movies and eating out, and having talks about the unfairness of teachers and the kindliness of friends.

I have watched their lives, been a joiner in their doings and a playmate in their fun. So, when Nathan asked me to join them, my heart leapt with joy! To be with these boys, both now 19 years old, was a privilege. To be asked to join them on an extended trip was an honor.

"I'll come!" I exuded. "Thank you for inviting me! I love your idea of where you want to travel and whatever you want to see is fine with me. We'll have such a grand time!"

It mattered not to me when. We would work it out. Or how long - days or weeks? We would figure it out. Happy exuberance was in the air. A big trip was in the making. Nathan, the organizer of lines and colors and, from age six on, a drawer of freehand maps, had a plan.

He wanted to explore the culture and history of the American West. "We will see the state capitols, visit sites of our U.S. Presidents, and take in the beauty of the landscape from state to state." Kenny and I will drive from North Carolina, making a diagonal line through six states, to Wisconsin, to pick up Nathan. Then the three of us will head west as far as Wyoming and Montana. We will cross over into the Canadian province of Manitoba to see the Royal Canadian Mint (Nathan is a collector of currency) and come back to the States through Ontario. We want to say that we have seen and said hello to our good neighbor to the north.

It's important to our mapmaker to set foot on as much geographical terrain as possible on this planet. The wide swath of states we will pass through will get him that much further in achieving this goal. In ten days we will put on six thousand miles in sixteen states and two provinces. Nathan also wants his good friend Kenny, who hasn't traveled west beyond Tennessee (except for a flight to California), to see these states for the first time. I, who am a seasoned traveler, will happily be in the company of these two eager young men who are ripe for adventure. And I am too.

# CHAPTER 2

# NORTH CAROLINA TO WISCONSIN

It is late afternoon on May 10th 2005. The sun streams full and warm. There is a vibrant lightness in the air as I pick up Kenny after his final exam. It could be the beginning of anything. I feel a space of sky and time, ready and ripe for a primordial hatching of the unknown.

With a stack of maps in the van, we head west on Interstate 40 in our Ford Passenger Van, two hundred years after Lewis and Clark made their uncharted venture west, by foot and by canoe. These explorers in 1804 and 1805 mapped a virgin territory for the rest of us to find our way to the Pacific coast. Kenny, Nathan and I will meander near and across some of their path when the three of us come to Missouri and the Dakotas. But now just the two of us are speeding along from the Carolinas' land of cotton to the dairy land state of Wisconsin.

Tall, slim Kenny has settled his agile frame into the passenger seat. With a sweet smile, he looks across the leather arm rests and says, "My tests are over. I'm really glad." He sinks further into the spacious, tan to match the van, seat.

"How do you think you did?" I ask.

"I think I passed," he grins in answer. Relief is showing on his unlined face.

"I'm so glad for you. This trip can be our celebration. School is over, and we're free and happy as can be! I am so pleased we are on our way," I exult.

"I'm glad too," he chimes in.

My travel companion is a pleasure to be with. He makes no demands, speaks softly but clearly, and is engaged with me at every moment with his kind, sparkling light brown eyes always ready to meet mine. He is a kind man who has thoughts and ideas tucked away for easy sharing when the time is right for everyone. I'm fond of this boy and I bubble with warmth as we put on miles into Virginia.

Kenny takes over the wheel as we slip into West Virginia and then quickly cross the state border into the Bluegrass State of Kentucky. There is still enough light in the sky to see the regal-looking, thoroughbred horses, neat white fences and rolling hills of cleanly-cut, green grass. Kenny is color blind to green, so he perceives the scene in his own unique way.

As the sky darkens, we pull into a motel parking lot in Lexington, Kentucky. The swimming pool is open! Kenny eagerly jumps in and does smooth laps and I do exercises in the neck deep water. After sitting so long, my body drinks in the stretches and movement and as I let go and float, all the muscle tension seeps away.

We want to meet Nathan tomorrow by noon and still have ground to cover, so we collapse into our separate beds and drift off into our separate worlds of sleep and dreams.

Early morning I steer my van back onto I-64. The highway seems quiet after the heavy hum and drum of speeding trucks last night. And it's quiet in our space. Kenny, in his white shorts and light blue T-shirt from yesterday, curls up on his seat to get more rest. These college kids are used to sleeping in daylight hours when I am rarin' to go. But, unlike many of the kids, Kenny doesn't need to have music vibrating from the speakers. I relish being with my thoughts.

We pass by Frankfort, the capital of Kentucky, and know that Nathan will want to see it on our return. In Nathan's nineteen years, he has chalked up being in thirteen state capitol buildings, well charted in his brain, along with numbers, figures, tables, calculations and systems for science, math, history, languages and almost any field of knowledge, filling all the neuronal places. And ready for instant retrieval like magic. There is good reason he was the captain of his high school's brain game team.

I cross the border into the distended rectangle of Indiana and head north on I-65. The land is flatter here. South of Indianapolis, the capital city to the Hoosiers, the transmission light comes on. I am alerted to a strange lack of response when I try to slow down or accelerate. It feels as though the engine gears are not engaged. This car was tuned up before we left, but something has gone wrong. "Kenny," I call over to the tousled blond head, now wedged between the seat back and the doorframe. "Sorry to wake you, but I think the transmission is giving up and I need to find a repair shop."

The landscape looks barren, as I pull off the highway, not hopeful for finding a car repair shop and at this early hour before eight. Remarkably I drive this faltering vehicle several miles and pull, like a magnet is drawing me, in front of a white shed. Kenny's and my eyes look in disbelief at a sign nailed onto the front wall. 'Beck Muffler and Transmission.' Franklin, Indiana. Fifteen minutes after we arrived, young Tom Beck, with weathered face and hands, opened his shop and set out to fix whatever ailed our car.

I knew we might be in for some hours of wait. By a considerable measure, Kenny is the most patient person I know. So, I restrained my usual urge to wonder, "How will I get to the next place in time? How could we meet Nathan by noon?" We settled into a room that was bare except for some plastic chairs. I looked over at the service desk in the hall and saw a sign and laughed out loud as I read it to Kenny. "Shall I rush your rush job before I start the rush job I was rushing when you rushed in?"

And he calmly said, "I don't mind waiting, however long it takes."

"Kenny," I praise him, "your patience is a good lesson for me."

There was more wisdom framed and tacked onto Beck's white stained wall. "If you always tell the truth you don't have to remember anything. - Mark Twain."

"That's the truth. I agree with that," said my wise travel companion.

And below that, in the same frame, by Twain, I read, "Life would be infinitely happier if we could be born at the age of eighty-eight and gradually approach eighteen."

"You're nineteen and I'm approaching seventy. What do you think Kenny?" I asked, still peering at the words.

"Age doesn't matter. Your age or mine."

"I agree with you. Age doesn't matter to either of us," I say. "I think Mark Twain is saying there is so much learning along the way, that we could have benefited from earlier or later in our lives, that it would be nice to live our lives again in reverse direction."

Two hours later, a blip on the script of both our lives, our van is fixed and Kenny drives us back onto I-65. He, the van and I are all re-infused with life.

"Kenny," I ask. "All these states that we're passing through, makes me wonder where would you want to live if you could choose anywhere in the world?"

"The ideal place for me to live," he answered, "would be on a tropical desert island with a few friends and a wife. No responsibilities, no worries and no stress."

"That sounds like Paradise," I say with a smile. "Though Paradise could be a little boring,"

"It wouldn't be boring to me," he says with certainty.

Now, Kenny, though a bright, playful, cheerful young man, is not what most would consider an achiever. If it's too hard to do he will not do it and he sees no need to do it. He doesn't see the long-term payoffs of any venture, including working to get a college degree or a skilled job apprentice license. He doesn't want to work (he's tried it) and he doesn't see the future benefits. He lives in the moment.

Our moments have passed into almost five hours as we skirt around Indianapolis, pass Lebanon and Lafayette, slip over the border into Illinois, with Chicago to our north, and finally cross the state line into Wisconsin.

# CHAPTER 3

# WISCONSIN TO THE MISSISSIPPI

With an earlier phone call from us, Nathan knew that we would be late, and we agreed to meet him outside the Campus Center of his college. "There's Nathan!" Kenny spotted him first. He's looking tall, four inches over six feet, his blond hair of early years now turned to brown. He's running toward us, with giant leaps, on the tree filled campus from his college dorm. We are all smiles with the reunion. I ask him and he lets me hug him. Nathan is not a hugger. He doesn't like the wrapping around of arms and physical pressure of intimacy with adults, family or friends. But with children he embraces so warmly it touches your heart. With Kenny there are just grins and Nathan exclaims, "We have to hurry to the art museum, before they close at 4:00, to see my exhibit for Japanese History and Culture class." They race ahead, Nathan, a couple of inches taller than Kenny, while I rush to keep up. I am full with joy to watch them poke and tease and run with the wind. They wait at the museum doors for me, and we go in and up to the second floor.

"Two friends of mine, Leslie and Bridget, and I worked together," Nathan explains, "going through the collections in the basements of the Anthropology Museum and the Art Museum, looking for good art and artifacts to combine into several glass cases. We all collaborated on setting up the exhibit."

The Japanese artifacts, that they chose and arranged in the showcases, capture us with their delicate beauty. China dolls dressed up as the emperor and empress of Japan serve as the centerpiece in one glass showcase, sharing space with sword hilts and small paintings. Nathan has painted Japanese characters on cards to describe various aspects of Japanese history and culture and set them throughout the display. Other glass cases show off other Japanese artifacts saved by archeologists and collectors through the centuries. The history, the language and the culture of Japan have all been a fascination for Nathan since he was ten and now it carries through for him as a major field of study.

We three walk together up and over the grassy Indian burial mounds. They were built hundreds of years ago by the Effigy Mound peoples, who are ancestors of the modern Ho-Chunk Nation. The mounds are spread around the campus green like punctuation humps. We pass magnolia trees in full bloom and red brick, vine-covered buildings, to the dining hall. Nathan introduces us to a few remaining students (exams are almost over) and we eat a quick supper. We want to get to Iowa tonight.

"Kenny and Nathan, we are it!" I exclaim, as the now three of us pile into the van. Nathan adds his luggage to the heap of scattered bags already on the floor.

"We-are-ad-ven-tur-ers," I call out. "Ravenous for new experiences, wouldn't you say?" I grin as I settle into the drivers' seat and take a good look at my seatmates.

"Heave ho, heave ho, it's off to play we go," Nathan's voice comes out loudly and deeply and Kenny and I both laugh.

We leave Wisconsin, as the sun is lowering in the sky, and slip across the border into Illinois. "What adventurers do you know?" I ask. "Magellan and Robinson Crusoe, to name a couple," they say.

"And Leif Erickson," Nathan adds, "in the year 1000 AD. Your possible Viking forebear, Grandma Ethel, he's in your Viking blood." Nathan, often the one to broaden the prevailing view, said, "After the Native Americans, and probably the Chinese, Leif discovered this land!"

As a Swede, I rejoice, "Yay for us Scandinavians! Kenny you have a little Nordic in you, too.

"Magellan and Leif sailed the ocean blue, outdoing you know who," I usurp what might have been Nathan's line.

He adds, "And another adventurer, just like us, Matsuo Basho, traveled around Japan in the 1700s, walking and visiting sacred places and other sites and cities and mountains in all seasons. And he created prose-annotated-poetry, called Haikai. The poetry part of it is called Haiku today. As for Kenny and me, ha! ha!, I don't know how much we might write in those notebooks that you gave us," he smiled wryly in my direction.

I had told the boys before the trip that it might be a good idea to keep a diary of their experiences and thoughts on our travel. It was useful just as a practice and who knew of what use it might be in the future. However, they seemed only half interested in the prospect.

"I have one more," I add, keeping the subject going, "and I'll save the hundreds more for another time, ha! ha!" echoing Nathan's jocularity. "Richard Halliburton, an American adventurer and writer, at the turn of the 20th century." I pause and say, "We are five years into the 21st century. Can you believe it?" My mind floats up momentarily to the stars outside our windows and to eternity and to the universe and other dimensions and why and how is it all here. "Halliburton had a deep knowledge of history, just like you, Nathan, and Halliburton's daring got him into dangerous situations. Does that sound familiar?" I'm pretty certain that the boys know what I'm thinking about here in the van. "Halliburton tried to cross the Pacific Ocean in a Chinese junk. They were caught in a storm and everyone was lost," I finished.

"Sho ga nai," Nathan responded in Japanese. "That's life."

Now these boys are smart, nice and loved by many. Nathan is wonderfully social, one of the best-known kids on his college campus, he says and I have seen it too, for his brain and for his 'niceness,' a word he uses. He is driven to achieve incredible things. Kenny is quietly social and so kind and knowing, and not driven to achieve much that we can see. He's on this trip to be with us. Whatever we do is fine with him.

But, to put an edge on it, Nathan and Kenny are on-the-edge kids. They are not afraid of danger. To some extent, that's an admirable trait and it hasn't gotten them into any big trouble. But, this fearlessness that they have in common sometimes does cause their parents concern. Kenny will leap off rocks with a drop twice his height. Nathan will go off by himself to climb mountains or camp in freezing weather, without telling anyone. Both boys swam to an island in the Bay while the tide was coming in and the sun was going down. Luckily they made it back. They don't see risks as dangers. For all I know, someday they may attempt to cross the Pacific in a Chinese junk.

"But, we're free spirits," they both exult.

"The Constitution and the Bill of Rights were written for a reason," argues Nathan, who quotes from those historic documents frequently, among friends, in his classes and in almost any discussion.

Now, I'll admit it, I'm an on-the-edge kid myself. I might not take the same risks that these kids do, but I do have a free spirit for adventure. And I understand their urges to be unfettered. My acceptance of them is in the air. They feel safe to tell me what they do and to know that they will not be chided. I might tell them what society commonly expects in situations and possible consequences to what I see as risky behavior and what might involve my own safety, especially if they ask. But I rarely tell them what to do or not do. As adults, they make their own choices, without any reprimanding or judging on my part. Kenny and Nathan feel that in the air.

The sun has long set and we cross the Mississippi River, the state border line, and find a Comfort Inn, right on the water, in Le

Claire, Iowa, to spend whatever is left of the night.

Our room is spacious, Kenny and Nathan agree, and "there are two television sets!" though we have no time or desire to watch, and "hurry, let's get to the pool," from Nathan.

There's an indoor pool here, and to our liking, it is empty of people.

"Yay," shout the boys. "This is perfect!"

We dim the room lights, and the water surface, lit from below, undulates eerily with colored ripples and shadow, as the boys dive in. I step in and soon am floating on my own bed of gentle waves. Nathan and Kenny are bonding again as friends, I'm happy to see. Their happiness and exuberance are catching in this almost fantasy water world we are sharing.

After the swim, the boys, still in their swimsuits, run off like Tom Sawyer and Huck Finn into the warm air and the dark night, to ceremoniously dip their hands in the main artery of the nation, the glorious Mississippi.

# CHAPTER 4

# IOWA

"We're in Iowa, guys, just in case your dreams put you someplace else," I called over to the boys, stretched out on their beds and just beginning to wake up with my deliberate noise. I had already quietly done my yoga stretches, taken a shower and eaten my instant oatmeal, hot water added from the coffee maker in the hospitality corner. We agreed last night – or was it this morning? – to set the alarm for 7am, and the buzzer was ready to go off any minute. "It's time!"

"What time is it?" Nathan protested. "The alarm didn't go off."

"Just 7:00. It's ready to ring."

"But it's not 7:00 yet if it didn't ring."

And just then the clock's alarm came to life.

Slowly they pulled themselves out of their beds and they too came alive. One after another, they quickly used the bathroom. Kenny came out dressed in yesterday's clothes, the same white shorts with blue shirt. And Nathan, not one to feel the need to dress for summer, had on his favorite long black cotton pants and orange knit shirt. No fuss, and, lickety-split, we were ready to go.

Breakfast is not a regular part of their day. For one thing they sleep past noon if they have no classes and they are used to staying up into the wee hours, playing games and emailing and text-messaging friends. When they have good reason to be up early, they are not hungry. When their systems are ready, we have plenty of food for eating in the van, whenever they or I want. We decided before this trip to not waste time with food stops. Drive-thrus are easy, fast and cheap for them. In contrast, I have my own healthy fare of nuts, fruits and flakes - a California diet, stashed in bags, enough to satisfy my hunger for the entire trip.

Kenny wants to drive at this early hour, and, with Nathan riding shotgun, he quickly steers us onto I-80 west. "Go west, young man, go west," I tell Kenny. "My Dad used to say that often for no good reason that I could figure. But I was amused as a kid and that was enough reason, I guess."

As we half circled Davenport, Kenny glanced over and offered, "The population of Davenport is just under 100,000."

"And the only place where the Mississippi runs solidly east to west," Nathan sleepily mumbles.

We picked up our own straight aim west toward Iowa City. Nathan is slow to wake up, so I reviewed our plan for the day, even though 'presidents' and 'capitols' are his territory.

"We are meeting up with two Presidents today," I loudly announce, like a tour guide, "three states and three capitols."

"And one territorial capitol," Nathan, fully awake now, calls out. Nathan is making a reclaim on his territory. "Iowa City was the Capitol of the Iowa Territory for about twenty years before statehood was declared in the mid 1800s, 166 years ago. Then Des Moines became the state capital."

"You know what we are doing this very moment?" I ask, leaning forward from the backseat.

"Driving this car," Kenny quickly answered.

"We are sharing the air and hearing our voices and seeing the corn fields barely sprouted on these prairies of the Ioway. They were the Indian residents in the 1600s when La Salle claimed the Mississippi Valley for France. Hence the French names – La Claire where we slept and the state capital of Des Moines meaning 'of the monks.' The Ioway left for other parts and in came the German settlers, from the more settled East Coast, in the 1800s," Nathan spieled off. "The land, suitable for agricultural pursuits, attracted the farmers and the Protestant sects of Amish and Mennonites. Those two groups made a show of dissidence and they still do today, with their white linen bonnets and wide brimmed straw hats."

"And the Anabaptists," I add. "I heard about that group when I was a kid and going to the Baptist Church. I thought that this unknown and unseen group, to me, was ANTI-Baptist and opposed everything that the real Baptists believed and stood for and that they were a group to avoid. When in fact their beliefs, I learned as a grown-up, influenced Baptist, as well as Quaker, thinking and action. They believed that when you are old enough to decide what you believe about God, you could be baptized. Most churches believed in infant baptism. But, in my dissident church, I was submerged in water in a baptismal, built into the church altar floor, when I was around eleven. No longer a babe, I was of viable age to form a belief about something and then to make a decision to act on my belief. That is something I respect the Baptists for. Allowing you to make your own decision about an important religious commitment. And I remember, guys, questioning, with a lot of intellectual and emotional discomfort at the time, 'do I really believe this?' The truth was I didn't really believe most of the doctrines and dogmas I was taught in that little Baptist Church. I was a dissident too!"

"Yay, for you," cheers Nathan.

"I'm glad you have dissident beliefs," chimes in Kenny.

"But all the pioneers and land seekers and settlers were more or less dissident," I continued. "They all were running away from something, religious oppression or typhoid or extreme poverty. My own forebears left Sweden for Wisconsin because life was too hard in their native land. My grandparents, in Sweden, lost their whole family of four small children to the plagues of the time - smallpox, cholera and pneumonia. Can you imagine the strength it took to go on after that loss? They had little food and little land to farm, to say nothing of the rulers demanding religious allegiance to the state religion. They wanted to be free from those restraints and to start over. We do get second chances."

The boys take this all in, looking at the just sprouting rich green fields of corn all around us with a strip of highway cutting through.

"This very moment, we are following the tracks, guys," I pick up the earlier thread, "of the first railroad in Iowa, called the Mississippi and Missouri. It chugged with a steam-engine from Davenport, the sofa-city we just left behind on the river, straight ahead west to Iowa City and beyond, between two of our favorite rivers.

"I love how those railroad names roll off the tongue. The Mississippi and Missouri. As a kid I knew almost all of them. The Chicago and Northwestern. The Southern Pacific. The Green Bay and Western.

"And my favorite, The Atchison, Topeka and the Santa Fe," I sang out to a tune I learned from my dad, starting high and skipping down the scale.

Kenny and Nathan responded with approval. "That's good."

"My dad Arvid, your great-grandfather, Nathan, was the Depot Agent and Telegrapher in my hometown. He was a much-respected man in town with a very responsible position. Railroads were the main avenue for moving goods and people. The telegram was how, among other uses, parents found out if their son, probably around your age, had died in the war. My Dad would personally deliver the news."

The boys take quiet notice. No draft is looming for them, but wars are still going on in Iraq and Afghanistan. Kenny and Nathan have seen the grim side of war in the news, both know people who are fighting, and they know that war can get you in the end.

"But on a happier note," I lighten up, "when I was as young as ten, I rode the Green Bay and Western freight train, with a passenger car at the end of a line of dozens of freight cars. I went alone or with a friend to the neighboring towns of my hometown, Whitehall And I had a free pass to anywhere on any trains in the United States, because of my dad. I've loved adventure ever since."

"Riding alone was a brave thing to do," Kenny says with a smile.

"Times were different then," I explain. "I felt safe and my parents weren't worried. My dad would see me board the train in the morning and he could telegraph the depot agent in the next town if he needed to. I would spend time in Independence or Blair or Alma Center, walking the streets and going into shops, and then board the 'freight' going the other direction home, in the afternoon. What a sense of freedom I had!

"And I really miss those railroads. Nathan, would you tell us sometime what happened to the railroads? I know that you know, but save it for later, please. We're too close to the President's house."

"Well, it was President Eisenhower," Nathan started, seeming to not hear my request to wait, "who signed the Federal Aid Highway Act of 1956."

"Wait, wait," I interjected. Nathan has a passion to let loose with a database of information at a moment's notice. "Let's talk about it another time," I urge. "Our exit is coming up."

We left the westward ribbon of I-80 and curved onto Parkside

Drive to the Herbert Hoover National Historic Site. For all our conversation, it was not yet 9:00 on this cool, overcast morning. Kenny pulled into the empty parking lot and we strode onto the flat, spacious grounds, scattered with oak trees and flowering bushes. The stretch was invigorating. We walked and walked, mostly on the boardwalks, which were spread out like a grid across two hundred acres.

There were postings, throughout, for a dozen safety measures – stay on walks, don't climb trees or fences, avoid creek banks, do not disturb animals, watch for poison ivy and ticks. The boys hardly noticed the signs, but they were models of decorum. We strolled past the blacksmith shop, not yet open, and around the corner to the schoolhouse, which Hoover attended as a boy. We looked through the windows at the simple desks and stools that fill the austere space, that was originally a Quaker meetinghouse, and then a public school.

"Did you know that Herbert Hoover was a Quaker?" I ask the boys and they nod yes. "Quakers are peaceful people and he was a Republican president in a time of peace. But, ironically, he signed a congressional resolution into law, making 'The Star-Spangled Banner,' rather than 'America the Beautiful,' our national anthem. You know the war motif – 'the rockets red glare, the bombs bursting in air'." I'm building up to a tune and the boys join in, with a little help from me, "O' say, does that Star-Spangled Banner yet wave... O'er the land of the free, and the home of the brave?"

"I think 'free' resonates with all of us," I say, while eyeing my free spirited companions, "but wars are in our history and there are probably more wars to come. In his favor, though, Hoover was determined to halt the arms race. He sought, unsuccessfully, to eliminate all bombers and chemical warfare. Can you imagine that today? No way! We are so hooked into this war-industrial complex and I'm sorry to say to you future caretakers of our country, I don't think there is a way out."

We trot back, past the horses, now outside the blacksmith shop, to the birthplace cottage, where there are signs of life unfolding. A woman guide, wearing a long-skirted, long-sleeved work dress from the mid-19th century, with a knitted shawl over her shoulders, opens the back door and shows us the simple, fourteen-by-twenty-foot, two-room, white frame cottage.

"Herbert Hoover was born here in 1874," she states, as we all look at the bare furnishings – a wooden cradle, a table and chairs and a four-poster bed, covered with a quilt of square-foot pieces of dark cotton fabric, pieced together like the squared-off wooden-path network outside. As she talks, I can see, from the muscle tension on Nathan's face and a rolling twist in his neck, that he has a lot to say, but he waits until we go out again onto the grass.

"Kenny, for your edification," Nathan begins as we slowly walk the path to the Quaker Meeting House, "President Herbert Hoover was a very moral man with good intentions. As commerce secretary, he fed Belgium after WWI and, in this country, helped victims of the Mississippi River flood. He believed in American individualism and at the same time wanted a 'kinder, gentler' capitalism. But, history has not been kind to Hoover, saddling him with the Great Depression."

"I know that he was one of our most unpopular presidents," Kenny interjects.

"When Hoover was Secretary of Commerce," Nathan continued, "he supposedly warned President Calvin Coolidge of a possible economic downturn, that Coolidge ignored. Coolidge's policies can be to blame more than anyone else's, for the advent of the depression. Hoover wasn't perfect by any means, but the blame put on him was far more than he deserved. The stock market crash happened only a year in office, after all. There's not much Hoover could have done even if he was an oracle and wanted to fix the problems. Hoover, following Coolidge's one term presidency, beat Governor Alfred E. Smith from New York, a Democrat, to win the Presidency in the election in 1928. In office, he initiated many reforms. He expanded civil service protection, canceled private oil leases on government land, and, I like this, he directed federal law enforcement officials to go after gangster-ridden Chicago, which lead to the arrest and conviction of Al Capone on tax charges.

"Grandma, when my brother and I were young, you took us on a trip on I-70 across Northern Wisconsin for a 'Gangster Day' tour. We saw the inside of Al Capone's summer refuge on Blueberry Lake and the hide-outs and shoot-outs with the FBI of others like

John Dillinger and Sam Giancana."

"I'd like to see those places sometime," Kenny says.

"Yes, yes, and you can make it happen sometime," I respond, intending to encourage his own initiative, "but, as we all know, there's no time or space on this trip."

"Because of Herbert Clark Hoover," Nathan continues, "we have millions more acres of parks and national forests. But Black Tuesday, on October 29, 1929, did him in. The stock market crashed and all his good works were forgotten. He did run for a second term and lost to Franklin Delano Roosevelt." Nathan was as charged up as he was when he began. "He left his presidency in public disgrace and in private anguish."

"Nathan," I said, "your favorite president, Harry Truman, befriended Hoover and gave him a job to help feed the starving victims of WWII and Truman changed the name, Boulder Dam, back to Hoover Dam."

"Truman invited him in secret, early in his term," Nathan said, qualifying any hint of Truman openly sanctioning the Republican Hoover's presidency.

"Maybe that was because Hoover, with Quaker modesty, didn't want attention given to his good works and public service," I responded.

We had long passed the Friends Meeting House - a temple of silence! - as we listened to Nathan's recitation of exact names, dates and historical events, coming out in a stream. Eventually quiet takes over for us and we climb the rise in the unspoiled prairie land to see the gravesite, where Herbert and his wife, Lou Henry Hoover are buried. Two slabs of marble sit side by side. The President's stone has no inscription of any kind, simply the name Herbert Hoover and the dates 1874-1964. He is given Quaker simplicity, again, after a life filled with dramatic events.

Nathan offers for all of us, "May he rest in peace."

We walk back quietly through the grounds to the Visitors Center and watch a film of Herbert Clark Hoover being inaugurated by William Howard Taft. Nathan called it, "Amazing and absolutely fun. For all the things going against our founding ideals and Constitution today it was very enlightening to see Hoover talk about those ideals on TV during the cold war - freedom of religion, freedom of the press, freedom of speech, within certain laws, and freedom of enterprise, within some socialist framework, and our need to concentrate on home. That rings so true today."

Walking back to our van, I ask, "And who was President Hoover's vice president, Nathan? I didn't see it anywhere and I know you know a lot of them."

"Vice President Charles Curtis," he quickly answers. "Never to be heard from again."

The skies are still overcast as Nathan takes the wheel. But it doesn't cast a spell on our good mood. A State capital is waiting for us, not far away, and our capitol expert pulls onto I-80 west, leaving West Branch and then Iowa City behind. We should make it to Des

Moines, the near-center of this state of Iowa, before noon.

We all grab a snack in the van of wild rice cakes. Nathan does a flex and roll with his right wrist as he holds it, his other hand firmly on the wheel. It's a graceful and sometimes repeated motion that seems to release pent-up energy.

"This wild rice probably came from northern Wisconsin, the old territory of the gangsters, or from just over the border into Minnesota and Canada," I say. "They're famous for it and it's shipped all over the world."

Nathan's hand is quiet now; his attention is on the road. Kenny, aware of everything going on around him and responsive to it with a soft smile, is just pleasantly going along for the ride.

"I just saw this in print," I continue. "We'll see it on the flags and banners coming up at the capitol, if we look. It's the motto of this good state of Iowa that we are in. And I don't even know the motto of my birth state, Wisconsin. Ha!"

"It's 'Forward'," Nathan interjected.

"I'm for that," I respond. "But I like Iowa's. 'Our liberties we prize and our rights we will maintain.' We could put that quote on a sticker on our van. Or maybe we should get a special order Iowa license plate," I chuckle.

"I agree with that," Kenny says. "I want my freedom. I don't want schools teaching me. I want to teach myself. If I was with someone I love, I wouldn't mind living in a tent."

"But Kenny," Nathan quickly pounces. "It's fine to want your freedom. I want it too. But you are not getting anywhere. You are failing at school. You don't have a way to make money. Even if you live in a tent, you wouldn't have enough to take care of yourself. That's failure. You need to study and pass your classes and get a degree in something. It hurts me that you are not working at anything."

I stay silent and let the chips fall where they may.

"I'll work at the things I want to work on," Kenny defends himself. "And I don't want someone telling me what to do."

And then, in defense of his friend, Nathan brings up again with passion, "The Constitution and the Bill of Rights were written for a reason. I defend that every day with what I say. That's why I carry them with me. Our freedoms are threatened all the time with laws and wars and religious fanaticism and adults telling us what to do."

Nathan does, indeed, carry copies of these documents folded in one of his pockets or in his billfold and he takes them out to read whenever he has occasion to defend against arrows that might be aimed his way.

"Des Moines is coming up," I change the subject. "The French explorers must have relished finding the isolation of new land, in naming it 'of the monks'."

"What's the population of Des Moines, Kenny?" I ask.

"In the 1998 Almanac it was 194,000. Now, in 2005, it is probably about the same," Kenny answers with quiet certainty. "I knew all the populations, rounded to thousands, of the big cities when I was around eleven years old."

Kenny showed a special talent for math in his early years. He could add up big numbers in his head in kindergarten. But his writing by his own testimony was bad - bad conceptually and bad in his penmanship.

"How did you learn the populations of the big cities?" I ask Kenny.

"I got the Almanac for Christmas and I just looked at the populations a lot because they were very interesting. And I remembered."

With a map in his head, Nathan has aimed us skillfully off I-80 onto 14th Street, crossing University Avenue, turning right on Grand Avenue, where he parks. There it is right across the street. Up on a hilltop sits a long sandstone rectangle with four copper covered domes added to each corner. Towering in the center of the capitol building we see the golden dome, and at the very top of a belvedere sits a golden lantern.

We could use the warmth of a lantern, as the air is chill, even on this twelfth day of May. So Kenny reaches for his light blue sweatshirt, to match his usual blue T-shirt, and Nathan extends a long arm back into the van to a bag on the floor, behind Kenny's seat, for his folded and lately-favored kon iro na yukata, meaning a royal blue robe, suitable for a Japanese emperor.

At the foot of the steep hill of the capitol steps, Nathan asks me to face Kenny on the sidewalk and to hold my right hand straight up and at a right angle to my body and to make a circle with the fingers of my left hand meeting the thumb. He proceeds to cross his own middle two fingers of his right hand and spread out the other two fingers. He tips his left hand down with two fingers spread out, another finger twisted horizontally behind them. I am slow to realize that we are making letters, a non-standard, pictographically-based sign language, as Nathan calls it, to spell out IOWA. Kenny, with my camera in hand, snapped the pose, Nathan and I smiling broadly.

The boys then sprint ahead of me and bound up the long sets of steps. Nathan's silk gown is flying behind him like a billowing sail in the wind.

I can see that they are racing and it looks like a pretty even match as they top the stairs at the six tall pillars in front of the entrance to the 1st floor. They wait until I catch up, both boys holding the doors, and we all go in.

We walk around the labyrinth of marble pillars and passageways on the first floor and see the Governor's office. I check and the Honorable Democratic Governor Thomas J. Vilsack is not in. Would he have seen us if he was in, I wonder? Kenny, me and my grandson - the Japanese emperor?

We head for the center of the capitol to see the dome. High overhead, it is a kaleidoscope of color and light, orange and white rectangles and circles. A small American flag is draped in the middle. Again the boys let loose and fly up more steps to the second level, where we are pleased with our timing. The legislature is in session.

Some are in the marble rotunda talking business and we mix a little and climb the circular staircases to the galleries on the third floor to view both the House and the Senate in their grand spaces. Desktop computers, landline and cell phones and small electronic number displays for the counting of votes, we speculate, are scattered across desktops. The government is working, we are glad to see.

We head back down, where I rest on a long oak bench under a mural, Westward. "The early pioneers are heading west in Blashfield's painting," I point out to the boys, "just like us."

In a flash of a minute, they take in the scene, then call to me, "Let's go," and we all three hurry down the 1500 steps to the Grand exit doors.

We scarcely notice all the monuments scattered on the capitol grounds. Monuments are standing to honor soldiers and sailors of past wars, and to President Lincoln and his son Tad. There's a miniature, exact replica of the Liberty Bell, gift of the federal government, and even a Japanese Bell and Bell House, given by the Japanese in thanks to Iowan farmers who gave them hogs and corn in the 1959 typhoons.

"Arigato gozaimashita, do itashimashite," calls Nathan, in flawless articulation and emphasis that a native of Japan would admire, "to the farmers and to the Japanese. Thank you, you're welcome." Nathan's Japanese yukata nagareru is flowing and shimmering with the run back to the van.

It's barely 1:00, but we still have a long ways to go before we sleep in Topeka tonight. From Des Moines to Independence, Missouri should take us less than three hours and we hurry and grab fast food on the way.

I pull into the drive-thru lane at Quiznos Subs, and wonder to myself what Lewis and Clark would think of all this. "A Turkey Sub, please, with lettuce and tomato, no cheese and a large Coke," Nathan calls across me to the microphone. Nathan chose at age eleven to not eat dairy because milk is for the calves and not humans. He can't always be sure about the dairy content of breads offered but he has checked on past visits to many places and he reads labels. He also decided at a young age to not eat smarter mammals, that category including beef cattle, deer and especially pigs and then he phased out all mammals for delineation's sake. It is not like eating Kosher, and though Nathan has one-quarter of his genetic inheritance from Jewish blood, it is not a religious thing for him. It is moral and dietary. He just wants those creatures, of whatever god, to live. Turkeys, chickens, salmon and tuna are a little more dispensable, he sees. Moreover, these are some of his favorite foods and thus are regular fare for him. But no octopus, please, since they're too smart. And if he knows that a creature is abused, he tries to find another source of protein. His eating is very conscious and intentional.

"I would like the Traditional Sub with everything and a large Coke, please," orders Kenny, open to any kind of food, through his open window in the back. "Three waters, no ice, please," I say, knowing that ice inhibits digestion. I move onto our highway heading south and reach for my can of nuts.

"That's the fourteenth state capital I've seen. I have a lot more to go," says Nathan, partially removing the paper wrap around his sub and taking a healthy sized bite.

"That's my twenty-first state," Kenny says, who is slowly and steadily working his way through our nation's states, as well as his beef, ham, turkey and cheddar sub. "What about you?" he asks me.

"Somewhere over forty states, I think," quickly calculating it in my head. "I don't know how many capitols. I've been around a lot longer than you guys and I still have a ways to go to see all fifty states."

"Nathan, name all the capitals," Kenny challenges.

And Nathan proceeds to say them all clearly, city first, then state, in a round-about geographical order, "Augusta, Maine. Concord, New Hampshire. Boston, Massachusetts." And on and on steadily, through all fifty, to finish with, "Cheyenne, Wyoming."

Nathan has demonstrated this feat in the past, but it is always fun to hear him rattle them off.

"We'll see Wyoming, but we don't have time to see Cheyenne, sad to say," Nathan looks at us with a clown 'sad sack' face and then he brightens, "Kenny, do you remember the populations of those capital cities?"

"I knew them all from the 1998 Almanac and the populations now are probably close to the same as then. I'll tell you as we see them. It would be boring now."

"Please finish telling us about what happened to the railroads," I ask Nathan, looking for abandoned tracks along I-35 and not seeing any.

"It was President Dwight D. Eisenhower who signed the Federal-Aid Highway Act of 1956 into law, from his hospital bed. It cost billions of dollars to construct interstate highways all over the U.S.A. He drew six lines, three horizontal and three vertical on a piece of paper and told his people to base their freeway system on it. The reason, he said, was for national defense. If we were invaded by a foreign power, the military would need good roads to be able to quickly transport troops around the country.

"What happened was that the Interstate System pretty much supplanted the railroads. They ceased to be as important in the modern age, as they were for the pioneers and explorers and settlers. So we can thank a Republican president for the largest public works project in American history up to that point and for the auf wiedersehen to the railroads."

"Adios a tu iron railway," Kenny says, with a lilt to each word. Though he's been to just sixteen states before this trip, he has been to Spain and his knowledge of Spanish slips out in a light tune.

I plead for one last tribute to the iron horse and sing:

"I've been workin' on the railroad,

All the live long day.

I've been workin' on the railroad,

Just to pass the time away."

The boys are listening with amusement, so I continue,

"Don't you hear the whistle blowing?

Rise up so early in the morn.

Don't you hear the captain shouting

Dinah, blow your horn?

Dinah, won't you blow," and the boys join in on a more familiar chorus,

"Dinah, won't you blow,

Dinah, won't you blow your hor-or-orn?

Dinah, won't you blow,

Dinah, won't you blow,

Dinah, won't you blow your horrrn?"

From my driver's perch, I'm looking around with exuberance at the fields of corn and soy and wheat, passing by, and we keep going with another stanza.

"Someone's in the kitchen with Dinah,

Someone's in the kitchen, I kno-o-o-o.

Someone's in the kitchen with Di-nahhhhhh," we stretch out the high sixth interval until we run out of steam.

"Strummin' on the old banjo.

Singin' Fee, fie, fiddle-e-i-o.

Fee, fie, fiddle-e-i-o-o-o-o,

Fee, fie fiddle—e-i-o-o,

Strummin' on the old banjo."

"That was such FUN! I'm glad you joined in," I exude. "I've sung that work song hundreds of times. In case you don't know, the workers who built the railroads were the Chinese coming from the west and German and Irish immigrants coming from the east.

"Your Great Grandfather Arvid was a railroad man," I repeat from this morning, glancing over at Nathan, "who played the mandolin in a dance band. And your Grandpa Carl played banjo. So we have just done honor to two great men."

"Yes," they both say in their respectful ways.

"And speaking of your forebears, Nathan, your Great-Great-Grandfather 'Long' Nels - he was very tall like you - was a novice researcher and inventor. On his farm in Jackson County, Wisconsin, he spent years doing experiments with water, troughs and buckets to try to prove perpetual motion. He has a couple of patents in his name."

"My father and I have an idea," Nathan injects, "for a space elevator. But the details would take too long to explain. Suffice to say, the perfect place for it would be in Ecuador."

"Well, scientific research and inventions are part of your heritage," I observe with a smile.

We are almost at the Missouri border when we see the small town of Lamoni to our right. I call out to Kenny, in the back seat, "I'm guessing that the population of Lamoni is 569."

"I don't know what it is," Kenny responds.

"Goodbye to the Eastern Goldfinch and the Wild Prairie

Rose," I say with sparkle in my voice. "Hello to the bluebird and the Hawthorn Blossom. This state, coming up in one minute, has dinosaur remains and missouriense is part of the name."

# CHAPTER 5

# MISSOURI

We see, in the still overcast distance, a big green rectangle with a half-circle added to the top to accommodate the big 'O' of MissOuri, with the Great Seal of Missouri inside the 'O.' I pull off the macadam ribbon to the gravel, and park. We all leap out, me with my disposable camera. It's state-line picture time! There the boys are in their standard black pants w/ orange shirt for Nathan, and blue sweatshirt w/ white shorts for Kenny. Each is standing in front of the high metal posts that are holding up the state sign. So tall and straight and handsome they are, and comfortable with the world, hands in their pockets, and looking directly in my camera's eye and the beauty of it makes my eyes well up with tears.

I love these boys. They are their own creation, unique to the core of their being. Their joie la vivre, their spirit, their kindness just touch my heart.

"Your turn, Kenny, if you want to drive," I say when we start back to the van. They catch a look at the dampness on my cheeks and I ask, "Please, let me give you guys a hug," and I reach over to give them each a quick embrace and they hug me back. "Thank you for being who you are," I manage to say.

I hand the keys to Kenny and he is at the wheel ready to go before Nathan and I finish belting ourselves in.

"Do you know anything about this state, Kenny?" I ask.

"I know that President Truman lived here most of his life."

"Mark Twain came from Hannibal," Nathan interjects. "It's that way," he points out his window in the back seat behind Kenny while I have a turn in the front passenger seat. "It's mostly east and a little south of us, right on the Mississippi River. But we won't be going there. Samuel Langhorne Clemens was his real name."

I think about Mark Twain, the pseudonym, and about the main characters in the books that he wrote, The Adventures of Tom Sawyer and Adventures of Huckleberry Finn. He modeled the character of Tom Sawyer on himself. Though Huck and Tom's violent acts are way more extreme than Nathan and Kenny would ever do, I am seeing traits of both Tom and Huck in these boys in the van with me. All four of them, alive in life and in the books, are adventurous, fun loving, resourceful, inventive and not enamored by authority. They are free and cannot be put in a box. And in my mind's eye, they all look alike.

Tom, separately, likes to make wild plans, but he wants to remain respectable and recognizes that there are rules. He takes the lead and dominates in all his projects. He can survive on his own wits. I see Nathan as Tom.

Kenny emulates Huck. Huck is thoughtful and intelligent, but he's still a boy. He is easily influenced by others, especially his friend Tom. He doesn't care what society expects. He does what he wants to do or not do based on what he believes is right. He breaks the rules. Even with no resources or support, Huck will survive. As will Kenny.

Huck says, at the end of his Adventures, that he intends to head west. And west is where we three, not walking like Huck and Tom but sitting in this conveyance on wheels, going seventy miles an hour, are heading. Except at the moment we are going south to get to Independence, home of President Harry S. Truman. In this 'you have got to show me' state that is bordered by eight other states, Missouri.

Missouri was named after the Missouria Indians, meaning 'town of the large canoes.' Both the Missouria of Missouri and the Ioway of Iowa were the Native Americans of the 1700s, living in lodges of bark for summer, cattail leaves for winter and buffalo hides for teepees when traveling. They were pre-dated by Indians as far back as 12,000 BC. And centuries before that, in Ethiopia, the cradle of the humanoids, grew our earliest known direct ancestors, 4,400,000 years ago.

Which takes us back to Missouri and even further back in history, 89 to 65 million years ago, when Hypsiberma missouriense, a 'duck-billed' dinosaur, took up residence here in this show-me state and then ended the Cretaceous Period in extinction. Glen Allen, population 100, is the town where the dinosaur was discovered, not far from the Mississippi.

"Too bad, we are not going to the state capitol in Jefferson City," Nathan rouses me out of my ancient times' reverie. "We would need an extra four hours, at least, to drive there and back. We don't have enough time."

"Is there ever enough time?" I ask the boys. And I wonder. For anything in this life? It goes by in a blip. Even 4.4 million years is a speck on Einstein's space-time curve. The only way to slow time up is to go faster. The closer we travel to the speed of light, the more time slows down. But, according to the laws of physics, time can never go backwards. So we are destined to only move forward, slow or fast, relentlessly, to our eventual demise. The End. Of our physical existence anyway.

"I disagree with the cliché, life is short," Nathan comments. "Time is what we make it. Both in terms of our psyche and our use of it.

"Jefferson City is in the middle of this state on the Missouri River," Nathan continues. "Named after, guess who, the third President of the United States, Thomas Jefferson, also the second Vice-President, a U.S. Secretary of State, Governor of Virginia, an architect and more. He also played the violin. I'm thinking about playing violin again. My Suzuki lessons haven't been put into practice by me for fourteen years. Mou ichido hajimeru koto ni kyoumi ga arimasu. That means that I have interest in starting once more."

"Good for you," I praise Nathan for his renewed interest, and then, still thinking about outracing time, I posit, "I wonder if we'll ever find out that something can exceed the speed of light. What do you think guys?" looking toward Kenny first, at the wheel.

"It's fifty-fifty," Kenny says in his always even-tempered, soft but clear and well-modulated voice, with a sweet earnest look on his face to match the sound, "because I'm not sure if Einstein was correct or not. I've thought about this before and I hoped that we could find something that goes faster than light. I have no idea if things can go faster than light and if the things can, I think that people will find out how to do it pretty soon."

"I hope for that, also," I agree. "What about you?" I ask, looking toward Nathan in the back seat.

"Sure, I think that there is a possibility," Nathan answers quickly. "I'd like to do it, as an adventurer and an explorer and as a physicist."

"Einstein considered himself to be as much a philosopher as a scientist," I say. "He changed the world through the power of his unconventional imagination. You can do it, too, guys. And Einstein played the violin."

"Yes, we can do it and I want to change the world for the good," Nathan agreed. "But I have something more to say about Thomas Jefferson. As President, in 1804, he sent Meriwether Lewis and William Clark up the Missouri River to explore the American West. They were told to search for the Northwest Passage from the mouth of the Missouri River at the Mississippi, north of St. Louis, to the Pacific Ocean and they did and they returned two years later. They discovered the headwaters of the Missouri River in Montana and learned and recorded knowledge of the land, Indian nations, animals, plants and minerals." And then, with an amused chuckle, he said, "Our route comes close to following their route."

"Call it the Nathan, Kenny & Ethel Expedition!" I exclaim. The boys smile with soft 'yeas.' "We'll be making a blip of a slip into Montana, too."

Through the northwestern corner of Missouri, we've passed cornfields, soybean and wheat fields and fruit orchards, all part of the northwestern prairie region. This prairie land is rich farm country, helping to feed a nation. Cotton is growing in this state too, but closer to the Mississippi. And Missouri is rich in useful minerals - especially lead, taking care of three-quarters of our country's needs and most of the world's. Yes, it doesn't just weigh us down or kill us - we do need lead for batteries, gas tanks, glass, soundproofing, ammunition, radiation shielding, pigments in paints and print and polishing. And there is zinc, coal, limestone, iron ores and clays, mostly just east and south of our path on I-35 to Independence. It's not just the dinosaur, which was fossilized. Or was it the dinosaurs, which turned into these now vital minerals? And, not only that, Missouri manufactures these natural resources into useful products. You could be totally self-sufficient in this state, no need to get supplies from anywhere else. But if you wanted to you could jump on a boat on the Mississippi or Missouri or board a train to the east or west, just for fun, like I did as a kid. And we three kids are guzzling up oil and gas, from those dinosaurs, in our fast-moving van, just for the fun of it, to see the 33$^{rd}$ President of the United States, Nathan's favorite, President Harry S. Truman.

"We are almost in Independence," says Kenny, seeing signs of urbanity on this quiet prairie in mid-afternoon. "Population 112,000, seven years ago and maybe less now," he offers without being asked.

"Good. Independence!" Nathan responds with a pun. "I like being independent."

Nathan, looking at the map, gives Kenny directions to Truman's Library. After a respectful silence in front of the library, Nathan points out that when he was in fourth grade, he and his brother, both in admiration of President Truman, dressed up as him for Halloween. I remember the photos of them with their oversize suits and glasses and earnest looks.

From such young roots of interest in this President, the building before us is almost like sacred territory for Nathan and then he bounds out of the van. Kenny and I catch up at the entrance and we all run down the stairs to the lower level and immerse ourselves in the exhibit, Harry S. Truman: His Life & Times.

Harry Truman, the people's president, (b.1884-d.1972) lived all of his years in Missouri, except for his ten years in the Senate and eight years in the White House. He was a farm boy, having grown up on a series of Missouri farms, and that's where his mother said he got his common sense. At age thirty-two in 1917, he fought as an army lieutenant in WWI in France, near the Swiss-German border. He returned in 1919 and married Bess, whom he had known since both were five years old. He tried his hand at haberdashery with a partner and failed. He loved books and the piano. Then he proudly declared that what he really wanted to be was a politician. He considered this a true profession. His interest was in good government.

"Look at this," I point out to Nathan in the collections of papers and documents and correspondence under glass. "Truman said, 'I would risk my reputation and my fortune with a professional politician sooner than I would with the banker or the businessman or the publisher of a daily paper! More young men and young women should fit themselves for politics and government'."

"That's one of the things that I admire about Truman," Nathan says. "He was a realist in the necessity of compromise in politics and he had a professional and altruistic belief in his reasons for entering politics and his work in government. And he encouraged us to be active in running our government at all levels."

"Today, we are so cynical about our elected officials," I say, "with all the lies, corruption, self-serving intentions and bickering that we hear about. It's hard to rise above that." I look at Nathan and plead, "Help us with this! What happened and how do we get out of it?"

"Let's resurrect Harry, the straight talker," he answered.

There was so much more to take in. Nathan joined Kenny in an alcove, looking at a wall chart of Truman's years in government. I read the captions under photographs of his early years, his family and his time in politics.

He was a judge for a decade, then a U.S. senator for another decade until 1944 when President Franklin Delano Roosevelt drafted him as his vice presidential running mate. They won easily. It was Truman's one term as Vice President and it was Roosevelt's fourth term as President.

For years, Roosevelt had been slowly committing us into WWII. Then Japan attacked Pearl Harbor on December 7, 1941, and Germany and Italy declared war on the United States four days later. We fought back. On the afternoon of April 12, 1945, Roosevelt said, "I have a terrific headache," and he died of a massive cerebral hemorrhage. Immediately, the new President Truman plunged into decision-making in the war. He announced the end of the war on Europe on May 8th. He met with Churchill and Stalin at the Potsdam Conference in Germany and then ordered the dropping of the atomic bombs on Hiroshima and Nagasaki. Japan surrendered on August 14, 1945.

"Nathan," I asked, as the three of us sat on a bench before heading up the stairs, "what do you think of Truman's decision to drop the atomic bombs?"

"For all my love of Japan, he did the right thing. He wanted to stop any further aggression from Japan and stop the destruction of soldiers and civilians," Nathan answered thoughtfully. "Obviously, it was a tough, hard decision for Truman and his advisors to make, but I support it. It was the best possible decision. The cities were chosen to maximize military destruction and minimize civilian deaths. With

Truman's intention to drop the atomic bombs, he got the Soviets to declare war against Japan, which they did on August 6<sup>th</sup>, 1945, the same day that the atomic bomb was dropped on Hiroshima. The atomic bombs caused Japan to surrender early and thus prevented Russia from controlling northern Japan. We never invaded Japan with soldiers, but we would have if we hadn't used the bombs, and there would have been far more deaths. Truman took responsibility and that's one of the reasons I respect and like him. He also had a strong commitment to peace and helping other countries. After the war he put huge amounts of money and work into rebuilding Europe and Japan. A source of pride for the Japanese people is that their country has never been invaded by any other country, even by the Mongols.  Both Japan and Europe have stayed our friends."

"When you were in Japan," Kenny spoke up, "did the people like you?"

"Yes. They still don't like that the bombing happened to them. But there is no ill feeling at all toward us. They are forgetting about it and moving on."

It was time for us to move on and we ran up the stairs to find ourselves in a large empty space with a wall of windows looking out onto the gravesites of the President and his wife Bess. We turned to the left and saw a bronze figure of a man, dressed in a bronze suit, standing alone in the spacious corner, where two light sandstone brick walls meet. He looked diminutive in this emptiness, I thought, but he was life-size and so real and honest and straightforward, it almost took us aback. The boys went up to him, greeted him and thanked him for being such a great man. Nathan put his left arm around his neck, draping his long hand down Truman's left shoulder and leaned into him casually like an old friend, with a big smile. Kenny put his right arm around Truman's neck, both boys' heads higher than the President's, and all so happy and proud. The uncommon common man befriended by two uncommon boys. I snapped the photo for history.

Outside, we walk a concrete path to the white marble slabs resting ten inches off the courtyard grounds. We have a moment of silence to honor the great man and lady and move on to our van. The Truman's other 'White House' is five blocks away and we want to make the last tour of the day at 4:30pm. But before we get into the van, Nathan holds up a postcard he has purchased of a grinning Truman, his arms raised triumphantly and holding the front page of a newspaper with the mistaken headline in big letters "DEWEY DEFEATS TRUMAN." We all smile for the camera that Nathan is holding in his other hand to snap a photo of the three of us plus a triumphant President.

The newly sprouted green grass yards of houses that we pass are filled with flowering crabapple and pink dogwood trees and shade trees and green bushes. There on the corner stands the stately, pristine, 19th century Victorian house where Bess was born and where the Truman's lived for fifty-three years of marriage. After her husband died, Bess stayed on for ten more years. She died at the age of ninety-seven.

Chrome chairs and a table sit in a simple kitchen, out of the 1940s. Their two upholstered arm chairs, sitting at an angle to each other, in a cozy space near the front of the house, is where they sat in the evening, with their reading and conversation. And behind a door near the entrance, perched on a rack, is Truman's own coat and hat. The three of us looked and looked at that coat and hat and were transported to the reality of his world. And it was time to get to Kansas.

Visiting the homes, libraries, lives and works of two Presidents in one day made us heady and almost giddy. With the bright hopefulness of Independence still shining, Nathan reminded us that he wants to be President some day. He would want to restore our freedoms of religion, the press, speech and enterprise, all within some socialist framework, ideals held high by Hoover. Those freedoms are being horribly compromised and threatened, he believes. Truman, he thinks, was absolutely amazing, truly an inspiration, and was the kind of President he wants to be. Kenny is inspired and so am I, not just by Truman, but also by Nathan's idealism and passion and aspiration.

Nathan is in the driver's seat. You can feel his mind-body charge. Like Truman, he is in a take-charge President's mode. We make tracks near the Missouri River, a state's width west of the Mississippi, where Lewis and Clark started their 'Route to the Pacific' in 1804. The Mississippi River that Mark Twain romanced, and where the boys ceremoniously immersed their hands and arms, deep into the water, in the late, dark night. What seems like many nights ago was really just one. Perhaps Nathan was right. Time is what we make of it.

We go west on I-70, a band of concrete rising just above the main streets of Kansas City, Missouri. "What is or was the population of this Kansas City, Kenny?" I ask.

"444,000," he calls to me in the backseat, "and it's probably about the same today."

# CHAPTER 6

# KANSAS

We cross the state border and the Kansas River into Kansas City, Kansas, population 143,000, according to Kenny. The Kansas state sign is ahead of us on I-70 but there is no pull-off on this overpass. I quickly open my passenger window and take a shot of the sign with my camera in the encroaching dusk. The capital 'K' stands out in the line of lower case letters, 'welcome to Kansas,' on the robin egg blue rectangle, rimmed with white. A huge sunflower blossom, with a large white center and short yellow petals, is spilling over the edges of the sign. This is the 'Sunflower State,' Kansas, named after the Kansa Indians, and a Sioux Indian term meaning 'south wind people.'

"We're in Kansas!" I exclaim. "It's a first time for all of us!"

We want to make it to Topeka, the state capital, before night falls. Our eyes are following the weaving Kansas River, also known as the Kaw River as it flows east and we roll west. The Kaw leads into the Missouri River just north of us. It was at this confluence of rivers that the Kaw or Kansa Indians lived two hundred years ago, a warlike people who hunted buffalo and lived in dome-homes covered with bark. Steamboats in the 1800s once navigated both rivers, exchanging goods back and forth from the east to the western frontier. For three days in June, in 1804, the Lewis and Clark expedition camped at the mouth of the Kaw River where it flows into the Missouri River at Kaw Point. The sky is darkening and raindrops are starting to fall, as we imagine their tents pitched below us and to our right. The bald eagles and pileated woodpeckers that they describe in their journals are still around but out of our view.

Nathan's thoughts are still with Truman, as he says, "After the Potsdam conference, Truman's optimism of Stalin faded. Stalin didn't honor their agreements and Truman could see that Stalin's intentions were to spread communism. So the cold war began and our isolationism ended forever. Truman then started giving aid to Turkey and Greece, because he didn't want them falling to Soviet communism. Truman, and his Secretary of State, George C. Marshall, also instituted the Marshall Plan to rebuild Europe, and to keep the Europeans as allies. During the year long Berlin Blockade, imposed by the Soviets, Truman started an airlift which helped the Berliners to survive and eventually gain their freedom. Truman also ended racial segregation in the military. In spite of his foreign policy successes, his popular support in this country was waning due to economic woes. His approval rating dropped from almost ninety percent in 1945 to a third of that in the Fall of 1946. When he ran for a second term in 1948, he was considered an underdog to Thomas E. Dewey. But Truman defied all the pundits and predictions. Just one month before the election he barnstormed the country with a railroad whistle-stop tour."

"Do you know what a whistle stop is?" I interjected. "It's a railroad station in a town small enough that it is not a regular stop for the train. The town depot agent flagged the train if he wanted them to stop for passengers or freight. The train engineer pulled the whistle cord to alert his locomotive engineer and the approaching town depot agent that they were making the stop. When my dad started out as a depot agent/telegrapher in smaller stations than Whitehall, he had to flag the train when he needed them to stop."

"Yes. Well, Truman and Bess and Margaret made many stops a day through twenty-seven states," Nathan picked up his thread. "The people responded in droves and shouted the famous 'Give 'em hell, Harry.' The entire press pre-empted the elections, giving it to Dewey. But of course, Truman had the last laugh - or grin - in the famous photo that I showed you both. He was elected on November 2, 1948. The electoral votes of our home state, North Carolina, went to Truman in that year and in 1944. After that four-year term, he decided not to run again. He and Bess were very happy to leave Washington and to return to their quiet home in Missouri.

"Now that our trip through Missouri is done, and I mean no offense by ignoring our current host Kansas," Nathan continues, "I was struck by the similarities between Missouri and North Carolina. There's the temperate climate, both in terms of people and temperature, the southern charm and an ideal combination of city and rural life. The cities in both states are not too big but are still very cosmopolitan. The biggest cities in each state, Charlotte and Kansas City, are important to the nation in terms of finance and commerce. As far as rural life goes, both states are made up of small farms. The big plantations of the typical 'Old South' were few and far between. Looking at their history, they seem remarkably similar. Although slavery used to be legal in both states, Missouri did not secede from the Union and the only reason that North Carolina did secede was because every single state bordering them, culminating in Virginia, seceded first. I do admit that both states do, even today, retain some racism, but it's far milder when compared with other southern states. This largely results from the small-farm nature of rural life. Most families either had no slaves or only a few, out of economic necessity. I can feel the independent free nature of both these states in the wind! In Missouri we have people like Lewis and Clark, Mark Twain and Harry Truman. One of my favorite composers is Scott Joplin, who broke the mold with his cheerful, energetic Ragtime music. When my family and I visited St. Louis about six years ago, my favorite site to see, far more even than the Gateway Arch, was Joplin's house, including his own piano and sheet music. It was interesting to me that right before we left his house, the curator said he was impressed with how we were so interested in Black History. My parents were engaged in a lively conversation with him, so they didn't take too much notice, but I thought that everybody should visit this house. I had simply considered Joplin an important piece of all human history. When it comes down to it, people of all races or ethnicities or whatever have contributed great things to the world. George Washington Carver, the inventor of over five hundred uses of the peanut, or the 'goober' as he called it, is another great example of 'Black History' that I would never consider just Black History."

"While we're on the subject of music," I expand, "Thelonius Monk, the jazz composer and pianist, was born and lived his early years in North Carolina along with many other jazz musicians whom I love and whose music I play on the piano, just as I do Scott Joplin's."

Nathan continues, "I've heard you play the rags. I only wish I had the same talent on the piano as people like Harry S. Truman and Ethel Erickson Radmer."

"Well, thank you Nathan," I responded, "for the compliment, and for putting me together with such an esteemed President."

"You're welcome. In North Carolina also," Nathan continued, "Blackbeard, the pirate, had his headquarters in Bath and Ocracoke. Great patriots like Andrew Jackson and James Knox Polk, respectively nicknamed Old Hickory and Young Hickory, were born in North Carolina. However, unlike Harry Truman, I have little respect for Jackson, since he instituted the Trail of Tears and the more general forced eviction from southern lands of the five civilized tribes: Cherokee, Chickasaw, Choctaw, Creek and Seminole. That said, the North Carolinians of that time, unlike their neighboring Georgians, Tennesseans and Alabamans, were a lot more tolerant. Some Cherokees were thus able to stay in parts of the mountains in North Carolina and are still there today."

It is raining steadily now and the sky is dark. Kansas is famous for tornados, in real life and from The Wizard of Oz.

"Nathan," I begin to reminisce, "I'm thinking of when you were one of the Wicked Witch's Guards, called a Winkie, in The Wizard of Oz at your high school. And you were the end of the yellow brick road holding the flowing yellow sheet of fabric over your head."

"I also was a magical gust of wind holding and blowing the menacing witch through the trees," Nathan reminds us.

"Where's that tornado now?" I kid both boys, looking out my side window, behind Nathan, into the scary dark.

"I want to see a tornado," Kenny exclaims, and Nathan and I join in too. Tornado chasing does seem like an activity these boys would truly relish.

"Somewhere over the rainbow," I start singing and the boys join in. "Way up high. There's a land that I heard of, once in a lullaby." We keep going, among us remembering most of the words, through two verses. "Where troubles melt like lemon drops, away above the chimney tops, that's wher-r-re you'll f-i-n-d me-ee," we stretch out to lengths and heights and chuckles. "So-mmm-whe-ere over the rain-bow. Why then oh why - can't I?" My sides are hurting with laughter.

A storm is brewing, as if on cue. "We want to see a tornado!" we called to the wind. The rain was coming down hard, and the lightening was flashing. At my urging for the safety of all three of us, Nathan reluctantly slowed the van down to a crawl. "Somewhere, over the black clouds," he sang, making it up, as the thunder crashed. Nathan's brain was on over-drive, making up words, and we jammed along. "There's a super cell. Where a cold front hits a warm front, and it's gonna' be Grand Hell." We all joined in on another verse, "Da Do Da Do Da Do Da Do Da Dee, Da Dee Da Dee Da Dee Da Dee Da Dee Da Dum Dum."

Heavy rain bulleted the pavement. We sloshed through and made it to Topeka. As it turned out, no tornados funneled us into the air. The first emerald city motel neon lights that we could see in the dark storm - Capital Center Inn - beckoned to our wild and crazy troupe of three.

With considerable relief, for us to have met Nature's power and to have remained intact, I check us into the motel. But the boys, still filled with excitement, find an Indiana Jones pinball machine in the game room off the lobby. They play with exuberance and energy to spare, as if charged from the electricity of the storm, at the end of a very long day.

Both Nathan and Kenny love to play with toys and they love games. They let loose with pure silliness and joy whether they are alone or together. Toys came first in their toddler years when they were alone in their own worlds. As they became more social in their middle school years they came to love the fun and competition of games.

I am remembering when my husband was alive and Nathan was five months old. Nathan was dedicated to making a toy work.

His Grandpa Carl was watching him and called excitedly to his mother (our daughter), "Look at what he's doing!" Nathan pressed resistant knobs and levers with great intensity and concentration until they finally responded. He was fascinated with objects rather than people.

And Kenny's coordination skills and balance that started to show in his early years in stacking cubes and leaping alone like a make believe Peter Pan are showing now in the pinball game with some competition from his best friend, Nathan.

I have already gone to our room, while Kenny continues to play pinball, and as Nathan goes off to explore the conference room and various lounges on the 1st floor. He often goes on adventures with Kenny and other friends through the woods in North Carolina, to take in the serenity and the beauty that nature offers there. This time, Nathan does not mind the total solitude and takes the time to sit down alone in the dark, empty conference room to ponder deep thoughts about his life, as he tells me later. Prime among these thoughts are the trip so far, his life at college and his trials and tribulations with girls his age. He is a man of reason, but nonetheless he has an emotional profundity to him too, that I have seen. He has told me that he can rationalize himself out of as strong an emotion as love, but at the same time tries to be dedicated and patient. Yet those same qualities, when the feelings are unrequited, have occasionally come across as too strong to a couple of young women. As he has been socially maturing, he has learned a lot, but he is still far from perfect, as he says it, on the dating scene.

After both boys are finally played out with their games and their private thoughts, we all collapse, totally exhausted, into our separate beds in our first floor room directly off the flooded parking lot. Bed never felt so good. Our first full day together has been so packed with action that it could have been a week. And we have more days to come! Sleep came quickly for all of us, along with dreams of the Winkies and tornados and presidents and capitols. Seeing the Kansas capitol building tomorrow will be a first for all of us.

We jumped out of bed early on Friday the 13th of May, survivors of good luck last night in a storm and no bad luck expected today. All three of us took rolls and fruit from the breakfast room and were out of the motel by 7:30am. The storm has passed, but we walk through streams of water to get to our van. The world looks very different today! For one thing, we can see. Last night was pitch dark with flashes of headlights, lightening and rain hitting the windshield and the neon signs of Topeka's outskirts.

Today we quickly get back onto I-70, and drive straight for the capitol. A gray stone building in the configuration of an X (a Greek cross it is called), with a green copper dome, sits on a flat piece of land. The portico that we are facing resembles, with less gravitas, the Parthenon of ancient Classical Greece. That temple on the Acropolis was built in the 5th century B.C. and is an enduring symbol of Athenian democracy, as is this Classical Revival capitol of Kansas, standing high for democracy. It holds the Senate, the House of Representatives and the Governor's office of governance, plus chambers for the Judiciary. There are eight pillars on the Parthenon temple of Athens. We count seven pillars on the portico in front of us. The boys race ahead of me up the steps to the top to locked doors - is it too early? And we come back down to a non-descript entrance at the bottom under the portico. The plain door is unlocked and we climb more steps inside to the second floor corridors to see the infamous (for their content and the disapproval of the legislature at the time) murals painted by the famous John Steuart Curry, a native of Kansas, (b1897-d1946). With all the roadblocks in the way of his creative expression, he refused to sign the murals and never completed the ones for the rotunda. Decades after his death the legislature apologized to his descendants. So we are intrigued.

The most controversial painting was of John Brown, an abolitionist, committed to keeping Kansas a free state by prohibiting slavery. He was also a murderer of five pro-slavery men. Throughout the corridor walls we see towering images of Kansas frontiersmen and Spanish explorers, of opposing forces with swords and the Bible, and of symbolic tornados and fire. It is a bit unsettling for all three of us that Curry didn't get his due for such powerful work. The good folk of Kansas did come around and keep Kansas a free state, ratifying a constitution prohibiting slavery in 1859. Slaves from the South came in the largest numbers of any state to the state of Kansas to become free. Nathan, Kenny and I have taken in enough of the capitol building and we whisk past the closed offices of the

Democratic Governor Kathleen Sebelius, and hurry down the stairs to the street and our van.

We make a fast-food stop at Wendy's, where I order a side salad of raw vegetables. I put the first forkful in my mouth and taste sugar - where did that come from? - my self-imposed no-no because it's not good for health, and immediately spit it out discretely into my napkin. As Kenny bites into his Old Fashioned Hamburger with everything, he looks over with admiration. For all his 'eating anything' mentality, he does appreciate my healthful eating practices.

Nathan fills the gas tank and Kenny drives. Within minutes, Topeka is behind us and we are back on the Kansas prairie. Much of Kansas is grassland and we couldn't see it behind us last night in the dark. Now going west the grasses are shimmering in the fields along I-70. Bluestem, Indian and dropseed help feed their enormous livestock industry. Thanks to the Mennonites, who brought the first seeds from Russia centuries ago, we see fields of turkey red, a drought-resistant strain of hard red winter wheat, a Kansas breadbasket to feed a nation. Further west we would see buffalo grass, sand reed and salt grasses. Where the grasses are not, the flowers are – sunflower, primrose, aster, clover, columbine, thistles and morning glory, all wild in this free state and a glory to behold. If we drove an hour to the Southeast, we would see a reserve with about two hundred bison that survived their free-roaming days in the Wild West. Back in the 1800s, there were forty million bison (also called American buffalos) roaming the plains. Now there are one hundred thousand in preserves and on private lands throughout the Great Plains states. Our good feelings for beauty, survival and rich resources, surge as we turn north onto Highway 77.

"There goes Abilene," I say, pointing west, "the boyhood home of President Dwight D. Eisenhower. It's only a half-hour away and we are passing it up with our heading north to Nebraska. No time, my friends. But let's do him a little homage anyway.

"I like Ike," I continue in the favorite slogan of his day. "Ike did a good thing in warning us about a too-powerful military-industrial complex. Do you guys have anything to say? How about you, Kenny?"

"We studied him in history class," Kenny responds. "He was a General and he commanded the forces in Europe in the Second World War. But I don't know about war. Should we be fighting or not?"

"Ah, are some wars necessary and others not?" I press him.

"I'm not sure. I wouldn't know about when we need to defend ourselves and when we should not be fighting in a war. It's too complicated to say."

"Japan attacked us in the Second World War," I say. "And Germany invaded our would-be allies and committed the Holocaust. So our leaders and the nation thought we had to fight back to protect others and ourselves.

"Unlike the war we are fighting right now in Iraq," I continue, "where we invaded the country. It gets a little hazy though, because a lot of terrorist groups operate throughout the Middle East, and some of those terrorists did blow up the World Trade Center. I don't think that wars are as clearly defined now as historians have described them in the past. In WWII we had moral reasons to stop Hitler's genocide of the Jews. But were there more peaceful means to rescue the Jews? The idealist in me wants to stop all wars. When you get to my core, I'm a pacifist like President Hoover."

We all let that settle into our thoughts. I could tell that Nathan's brain was somewhere else than with Eisenhower, so I asked the boys to look out our left windows.

"Way west of here," I point to my left, "about four hundred miles away, just this side of the Kansas-Colorado border, is Mount Sunflower, four-thousand feet in elevation. It is the beginning of the gradual rise of the land to the Rocky Mountains further west.

"Eisenhower," I return to Kansas's most famous resident, "was the next President after Truman. And like Nathan said before, he began the Interstate Highway System, which we have been speeding on since we began this trip. Nathan, please give us some final succinct points about Eisenhower before we let him go."

"David Dwight Eisenhower, his birth name, was a Republican president, serving two terms," Nathan responds instantly with energy. "Under his leadership we had a cease-fire of the Korean War, and nuclear weapons became a defense priority. He expanded Social Security but kept a conservative economic policy. He proclaimed the 'Eisenhower Doctrine' in 1957, protecting Western interests in the

Middle East. This policy led to American support of dictatorships in the Persian Gulf, most of which are still supported by the U.S. today. This led to the kind of resentment and anti-Americanism that we see in the Middle East. He supported the Supreme Court decision that said that segregated schools were unconstitutional, by insisting that the District of Columbia schools be desegregated immediately. He proposed and signed into law the Civil Rights Acts of 1957 and 1960. Richard Nixon was his Vice President over two terms. John F. Kennedy became president, following Eisenhower, in January 1961." Nathan was done and he looked over at us with a smile of satisfaction.

"Thank you, resident historian," I smile back. "That gives such a clear picture of events. Forget history class. Right, Kenny?"

"Yes, I don't like classes. They are boring and I don't want to work in them so I don't go. I like to get my knowledge in other ways."

"Well, you're in the right place!" I exult. "And we are also about 200 miles east of the approximate geographic center of the lower 48 states. It's on a pig farm. We are in the center of the country, if not the center of the universe."

"What do you mean by 'geographic center'?" Kenny asks me.

"It usually means the mathematical center of the total land area. One method is to cut the shape of the country out of cardboard and balance it on a pin until it balances horizontally in all directions. In this case, the pin is on the pig farm."

"I don't think it matters," Nathan dissents. "I believe a much more important location is the geographic center of North America, which is located approximately in North Dakota. We can't ignore Mexico, Canada and Central America. They're all vital to our economy, culture and society."

Kenny spots a sign on the roof of a silver metal shed in a grassy pasture ahead and reads it.

No God No Peace

Know God Know Peace

"We'd have to define 'god' and 'peace' before I could give those phrases any credence," I say.

"This is a state where some people want to teach creationism in school," Nathan says. "Many Kansans seem to love John Brown and anti-science."

"The state border is coming up, guys. No more Kansas. Welcome Nebraska!"

Nathan taps his heels three times, as if he were wearing Dorothy's ruby slippers. "Goodbye, maybe forever, to Tornado peaks, a! Which, by the way, you can shorten to 'Topeka'."

"Population 121,000," Kenny says softly toward his window to the west.

# CHAPTER 7

# NEBRASKA

Nebraska welcomes us with a simple grass-green sign with white letters - NEBRASKA...the good life. Tacked to the bottom is a small rectangle with the words, Home of Arbor Day. It's state line photo time, and we leap out and stretch and run across the flat endless field of early sprouted grass. A bank of trees is on the distant horizon. After the run the boys are firmly planted now in front of the metal posts, as I snap them in what seems like an eternal space of green.

"Willa Cather, the famous novelist, lived in this state," I tell the boys as we walk back to the van. "She was born in the late 1800s and her writing was inspired by the prairie land that fills this state. I love her books and I've read most of them. My favorites are O Pioneers, My Antonia, Song of the Lark and One of Ours, about a young Nebraskan soldier going to war, for which she won the Pulitzer Prize. Thank goodness you boys are not going to war."

"I haven't read her books," Nathan says and Kenny adds, "I think I saw the TV movie, O Pioneers."

We're rolling north on Highway 77, and corn and wheat fields are stretched out to the sky.

"In another hour we'll be in Lincoln, capital of this good state, and then on to Omaha." I say. And summoning up some history of this flat rectangle of a state, I add, "In the 1800s this was the land of fur traders, French explorers, missionaries and Native Americans. The Pawnee, Sioux and Cheyenne Tribes almost died off with the white man's smallpox, cholera and tuberculosis. It was home to the Union Pacific Railroad that followed the Platte River all across Nebraska. Land was given away by the Federal government to bring in settlers, with the Homestead Act of 1862. Today farmers and ranchers produce grain and meat on almost every inch of the land in this state. And, as you know, Nebraska produced a President, Gerald R. Ford, born in Omaha."

"Kenny, what do you know about Ford?" asks Nathan.

"I know that he was Republican and he was in office just before President Jimmy Carter and before President Reagan," Kenny offers. "I know what he looks like. He was sort of thin with grayish hair."

"That's right," Nathan assents. "He was born Leslie King, Jr. and then took on the name of his stepfather, Gerald Rudolph Ford, Jr. When Nixon resigned in disgrace, Vice President Ford took over in 1974 for one term as the 38th President. Nelson Aldrich Rockefeller became the Nation's first unelected Vice President. Ford pardoned Nixon and probably lost the election to Carter in 1976 because of it. During Ford's presidency, the Vietnam War ended, the United States celebrated its Bicentennial and the nation healed from the impeachment trauma."

That seemed to be enough to say and we settled into silence, watching the fields of grain go by and some birds flying high in the gray sky. Perhaps some of them are eagles, I thought, though the one thousand bald eagles recently counted in the valleys of the Platte and Missouri Rivers have probably migrated north by now to Canada for the summer. Water tributaries are all around us including the Big Blue River just to our left. Fish is the bald eagle's main source of food. Their keen eyesight is eight times more powerful than mine and I imagine them seeing their prey under the water and diving for it like a pelican and then perhaps seeing our heads in this van. The wooly mammoths have long gone. They roamed these plains half a million years ago during the ice age. The boys stay quiet with their own thoughts and gaze at the landscape.

Rising from our reverie, a city is quickly upon us. Lincoln, named after the Great Emancipator himself, lies in a basin. Rivers converge here, as they do in many cities, and nourish the soil and quench parched life. Highway 77 takes us along meandering Salt Creek and then we are there. A towering capital building is in front of us, unlike any that we have seen. Two long low wings of limestone are stretched out for several hundred feet with a skyscraper in the center. The tower reminds me of the Empire State Building, with its narrowing tiers, topped with a round dome and a spire to the heavens. But, we are in Middle America looking up 400 feet to a gold-glazed dome topped by a bronze statue of a man sowing grain. The architect, Bertram Grosvenor Goodhue, was inspired by Art Deco, and helped launch the American Modernism design movement in the early 20th century.

"I love architecture," I tell the boys. "In my youth I wanted to be an architect, along with a dozen other professions. My first two years of college were in Chicago and I saw the German Bauhaus style of architecture in the functional cubic boxes downtown. This purely decorative Art Deco style that we are looking at is a big contrast to Bauhaus."

We enter the capitol, climb a long flight of stairs to a single set of doors and step into what seems like a castle. Arch upon arch of limestone and glass are rising majestically to a ceiling of mosaics. The mosaics, murals and paintings, filling this vestibule space, showcase the state's Native American and agrarian heritage. Busts of soldiers and hunters, poets and novelists fill the corridors.

This representation of the past is serving as a theatrical backdrop for a ceremony happening in the center of the capitol building. What unexpected good timing for us! Hundreds of people are gathered to watch Native Americans dance in full costume to the music of drums, flutes, gourd rattles, bells and whistles. We catch the spirit and move to the rhythm as we continue to climb more steps. Nathan and Kenny prance ahead of me, like the Indians on their 'Big Dogs' (horses), caught and stolen from the settlers of a couple of centuries ago. America's horses were originally shipped over by the Spaniards in the 1500s. The white man took over the Indian's land and killed their buffalo, bringing on the ensuing Indian wars. Some of that history might be part of the ceremony that we are seeing today.

We pass the Governor's office and hear that Republican Governor Dave Heineman is not in. We have no time for a visit anyway. We have a lot more ground to cover today and it is already early in the afternoon. We hurry on.

As we look back at the tower center of the capitol, Nathan observes, "It looks like Chimney Rock in the western part of this state. The pioneers on the Oregon Trail would pass it in their Conestoga wagons. It serves as a geological masterpiece, just as this capitol serves as an architectural one." We imagine Chimney Rock as a rocky spire with tiers, thrusting above the flat prairie land into the sky, a landmark that inspirits and guides the pioneers of yore.

The boys grab a bite to eat at Burger King, with Kenny supporting the beef industry of this state and Nathan the fish from the rivers. We pick up I-80 for a quick ride into Omaha.

"Thanks to the recommendation of a college friend, we're off to the zoo!" exclaims Nathan.

"Yayyy!!" Kenny and I shout.

"No Presidential stop today," I say. "Gerald Ford's birthplace in Omaha is burned to the ground anyway, decades ago, so what's to see? Nathan has given us enough history to do him homage. And you guys do not know, but I have seen President Ford and Betty Ford, up close, in Palm Springs, about six years ago. They seemed like very nice people."

"Good for you," Nathan teases me. "My father saw him also when he was a student at the University of Chicago."

The zoo was on Nathan's itinerary when he planned this trip. It seemed like a good respite from government and history and geography. I have always made a point of seeing zoos in my travels to other countries, including seeing up close, with little fencing, the illusive Bengal tiger in India. The boys like to mimic animals, and with the mention of the zoo, they make unusual sounds in the van as we move along. Guttural, high-pitched, mish-mashing in the mouth, squeaks and squawks. I laugh uproariously and add a few barks and snarls of my own. There are no social faux pas here. "Ahkarrrggrrggrrrahrrroowoworrerranayyynaaeighghgh" come out from both boys in a fantasy torrent of lions, bears, baboons and zebras. It's a free state zone.

Nathan, I know, in his younger days, was so into his own world that he had no awareness of social blunders and he had to be shown and taught on many occasions some social graces. And Kenny, to a lesser extent, was clueless about what 'normal' behavior was. They both are more astute now about society's expectations, but they look for the chance to release the repressed urges in playful ways.

Continuing the exaggerated noises, I ask Kenny, "In this Nebraska land of open space – wheeee!! - and very few people – ahhhhhmm!!, give us the stats for what's behind and what's ahead."

In a low, nasal, computer monotone he tells us, "The-pop-u-la-tion-for-Lin-coln-is-two-hun-dred-and-three-thou-sand-and-and-for-O-ma-ha-to-come-is-three-hun-dred-for-ty-five-thou-sand."

"That must be about the entire population of this sparse state," I suggest.

In fact, the two cities make up one-third of the total number of people living in all of Nebraska, previously known as the Nebraska Territory.

"Ak-Sar-Ben," says Nathan, meaning Nebraska spelled backwards. He loves to play with words, twisting them, turning them upside down, creating puzzles and leaving it up to us to figure it out.

Omaha, or Aham-o, as Nathan says, is just ahead, named after the Omaha Indians who used to live here. They were forced to give up their land to the settlers, a couple of centuries ago. We head straight to the huge triangle of the Henry Doorly Zoo. This is the biggest attraction in the whole state, according to the zookeepers.

We cheer when we see that the orangutans are the first forest of creatures on the triangle trail. Orangutans - other spellings are correct too, Nathan tells us - are a favorite for all of us, because they are so smart. One Harvard researcher, psychologist James Lee, reports that they have higher learning and problem solving ability than the chimpanzee, which is our closest living relative. They have long arms, like mine, that reach and grab branches effortlessly, and I extend mine to show the boys. But Nathan's arms are longer than mine. Kenny, who is very agile and lithe, and is showing it with his leaps and jumps off a rocky wall, says that he wishes he had more of their acrobatic skills, climbing and swinging from trees. We have the family Hominidae in common with this reddish-brown ape. The orangutan's genus Pongo sets him apart from us about 30 million years ago.

"They are orange, as in orang-u-tans. I like orange," Nathan reminds us as we look at his orange shirt and his orange socks, almost hidden under his long black pants.

"The orangutans live in the trees," I say to Kenny. "Does that appeal to you, Tarzan?"

"Yes, but a tent is warmer," he answers with a smile. "I like how they look tropical."

"They're from the rainforests of Sumatra and Borneo, also known as Kalimantan.  So that is right on the equator, which just might be tropical," Nathan jokes.

My daughter later tells me that 'orangutan' literally means 'man of the woods' in the Malay and Bahasa Indonesia languages.

"Look!" Nathan is laughing. "The orang-U-tans are laughing! See the ones that are chasing each other?" he points. "You can see it with their grins and hear the breathing and panting sounds. Chimps and gorillas laugh too. Jane Goodall documented it."

Kenny and Nathan are both jumping now and running in circles and laughing with our good fortune – to be here and to see the apes first! Acting like apes makes us feel we're in our element. We are entranced with the noises - the craziness, the gaggles and guffaws and the raucous behavior. My wild travel companions and I and these wild apes clearly share the same animal kingdom.

The Cat Complex is next on the trail. The leopard, with its beauteous face and steady eye, is from the genus Panthera, as are the lion, tiger, jaguar and of course panther.

"Hey, guys," I say. "This leopard guy is your kind of cat. They can run faster in bursts than any cat. They can leap twenty feet and jump ten feet straight up - try that Kenny - and they can swim! And they sleep in the trees."

"And they stalk and pounce and go for the throat to kill," Nathan adds.

Down the path are the Siberian tigers, twice as big as the leopard. "Nathan, they're your color, too," Kenny says. "Orange all over with stripes that are black, like your pants."

"Hear those 'chuffle' noises?" Nathan alerts us. "They are to greet – to say 'hi.' Their growls are to claim territory. The roars are to give warning. Small cats can't roar."

"What's 'chuffle'?" asks Kenny.

"Small cats," Nathan answers, "can purr nonstop. Big cats can purr out but not in. That gap makes for what zoo people call a 'chuffle'."

The fabled lion, next door, is pacing and gazing and seeming to put us on notice. He carries himself like a king. He exudes strength. We sense that he might fiercely pounce on us in a second if the moat were not between us. Aggression is his nature.

"He's not the cowardly lion of The Wizard of Oz," I comment.

"No," Nathan says. "I don't want to imbue the real lion with weak human traits. The Swahili word for lion is simba. It means king and strong and aggressive. But, as a human, I like taking on the strong traits of the lion. You're lionhearted if you are brave. But it is a rare person I would lionize - for now, maybe Truman. But that doesn't make us better than each other. Remember, Truman was the common man."

"You're as egalitarian as they come, Nathan," I add, thinking of how this generous young college student includes everyone in on so many plans and how he is as friendly and conversational with the cleaning woman, whose name he knows, in his dorm as he is to all the students. "You treat all people equally and with respect. And I'm with you on your being inclusive, not exclusive. I do not idolize anyone. No putting anyone on a precipice."

"I think you mean 'pedestal,' Grandma," shot back Nathan, "unless you're wanting to push them over the precipice. Anyway, later we'll be seeing four more presidents on a certain precipice in South Dakota."

We all laugh and the boys take off on a near-lion's run – 360 feet in six seconds, to see the gorillas in Gorilla Valley, where the gorillas roam free and the visitors are captive in a window-lined tunnel.

"It's all relative and it's an illusion," I, ever the philosopher, say to my close buddies, as we enter this confined space and begin to look out on the seemingly limitless savannah. "We are more or less trapped in here. I'm glad none of us is claustrophobic. Do you think the gorillas think they're free?"

"They're deceived and deluded," Nathan says. "But they are endangered in the wild, along with many of the big cats and apes, so conservation is part of many zoos' agenda."

"And more and more animals are becoming extinct," I add. "It's likely just a question of how long it will take."

Kenny feels the pain of this notion by blurting out, "I feel sorry for them all and for us who will not always have them around."

"Well, we'll have them in zoos, as long as we can keep propagating them. But who knows. We're not doing very well with the frogs in the swamps of Florida. They seem to have lost their ability to have progeny. And besides that, a killer fungus is on the loose that could wipe out all the frogs in the world."

This bold-looking ape, a gorgeous silverback leader of the genus Gorilla and the tribe Gorillini, is the largest of the primates, including us. Gorillas are from the forests of Africa and the next closest relative to humans after the chimps. Like humans, they prefer the ground to the trees. The silverback is standing upright and the rest are sitting on their haunches or knuckle-walking on all fours.

"Gorillas are my favorite animal," Kenny tells us. "I like that they are friendly to other gorillas."

We see them chomping on bananas, apples, oranges, carrots and leafy branches. Judging by the intensity of their focus, eating seems to be a big pleasure for them.

"This is my kind of animal!" I exclaim. "They are vegetarian! And that is my kind of eating – including all kinds of leaves! Shall I join them for lunch?"

"Go ahead. They are peaceful and family-loving like you," says Kenny.

The three of us exit the tunnel to the light and a sense of freedom again and take flight through the Aviary to catch a radiant view of the flamingos, one of Kenny's favorite birds.

Kenny and Nathan take giant strides past the emus, on their way to Pachyderm Hill where the African elephants reside. I have a special fondness for this intelligent giant of the land mammals.

"They fondle the bones of their deceased relatives with their very sensitive trunks," I say to the boys. "They have a memory. What a remarkable thing!"

"Don't you remember, Ethel," Kenny chuckles, "that an elephant never forgets?"

In fact their everyday working memory of individuals in a party of twenty or thirty relatives is way better than ours. They can update and delete things rather than filling up a long-term memory bank. But they do remember those bones from years before. And a keen sense of smell enhances their recall.

"Those tusks are heavy," I say, looking at the ivory luster. "They could be 200 pounds apiece. But please no ivory poachers! God's creation needs those for foraging food and for fighting off invaders."

"Their ivory tusks are really their extremely large incisor teeth," Nathan says. "Our 'ivories' are enamel, as are the teeth of most mammals."

I wonder if there is any ivory in the rhino's horns, as we pass the white rhinoceroses, the other pachyderm sharing the hill. Both elephant and rhino are thick skinned and hoofed and share a muddy gray color, in spite of the rhino's name, and they are both killed in the wild for their tusks and horns. The horns in fact are made of keratin as in fingernails and are not ivory but are poached to grind up for Chinese herbal medicine.

"All elephants and rhinoceroses are herbivores," I say. "It's not just the gorillas. Their ivories serve them well for grinding all the vegetation that they eat."

We pick up our pace and loop around the lagoon filled with koi (glorified carp) that the Japanese call 'living flowers' as they breed them for color. We look up to see exotic birds in flight, as colorful as the koi flashing through water. Nathan loves the 'flying colors' of the parrots and their kin. Kenny claims his favorites are the parrots, as well as the toucans, and – oh yeah – the flamingoes from earlier on the trail.

South of the Garden, another cat surprises us because it is away from the Cat Complex. The cheetah, a solitary cat, is sometimes mistaken for the leopard with its coat of tan with black spots and its human size. The cheetah, unlike the leopard and lion and tiger, is not of the genus Panthera, but of his own genus Acinonyxis. He is the fastest of all land animals. At 70 mph he may even be able to keep up with our van on the interstate. They can make good use of their own big space in Cheetah Valley, though their roots are in Africa and ours are too.

"What do you say, we hop in the van and find some fast food," I say. "I've had enough of being trapped in a zoo and I long for the freedom of the wild."

"How about the Wild West?" Nathan asks. "Because, that's where we're headed."

I laugh and then pick up on our earlier talk about animal extinction.

"Kenny," I say. "For the animals that become extinct in the wild, living in a zoo is not the same, as I'm sure you know. In the wild, you don't let your survival instincts atrophy. Hunger, for one."

We forage for food along a strip of restaurants and find a KFC. I order my favorite comfort food, mashed potatoes, sans gravy, and corn on the cob, from the freezer to the grill – a veritable feast for me. Both boys order the Original Recipe chicken - no intelligent animal consumption here.

"When I was around two," Nathan said with a smile, "I had a phase of eating only orange-colored food."

"Like what?" Kenny asked, starting to eat his golden brown drumstick.

"Salmon, carrots, oranges, tangerines and the orange outside of Gouda cheese," Nathan named off.

"Why do you think you did that?" Kenny wondered.

"I liked orange," Nathan said, as if that answered any further questions. But then he added, "Some of the best tasting foods were orange. And I liked categories. They were fun and nice. I liked to look at everything at the same time in an easy fashion. It felt comfortable, but I did not feel compelled to do it, in case you wonder. I ended up leaving the orange diet after I realized that I liked so many non-orange colored foods. Like red strawberries, blue blueberries and brown fried chicken."

"Yummy," Kenny said, licking his lips after taking another bite of his fried chicken.

But was there even more going on in Nathan's toddler brain? His mother remembers that he was determined to eat only orange food, refusing other colors. Perhaps it was part of trying to make his chaotic world of choices more manageable and comfortable. And now he has a complex system of food that he will eat and not eat, based on healthful and ethical concerns.

It doesn't take us long to finish eating our yellow-brown color range of food and we are back on the road.

The Missouri River has joined us again right here in Omaha and along with it the legendary Lewis and Clark Trail. We cross the Big Muddy, filled with silt, west to east, and follow it north on I-29.

"See the Wide Missouri, guys?" I ask. "It was a lot wider when Lewis and Clark measured the river exactly two-hundred years ago.

And do you know why? I have a culprit!"

"The Army Corps of Engineers!" Nathan quickly pipes up. He remembers from comments that I've made, in past years, that I do not think well of the 'accomplishments' of the Army Corps of Engineers.

"Yes," I nod my head. "They tampered with nature and exercised what I call 'guy power' by building wing dikes and levees to control the flow, for whatever reasons they have rationalized through the decades. The river could no longer spread out like it did naturally a couple of hundred years ago. And do you know the havoc that created?"

I'm on a rant now, my feminist as well as my 'let nature be' leanings showing, and I don't wait for an answer.

"It caused flooding, for one, because it forced the water levels higher. And fluctuating water height made for declines in river wildlife – fish, birds and vegetation. Power is the name of the game."

"I wish that they had left it alone," Kenny, the back-to-nature guy, thoughtfully says, looking at me and then longingly toward the river. "Why did they do it?"

"To control flooding. Isn't that ironic? And to control navigation and irrigation. Control and power is the name of the game."

"We have to work at balancing out progress - our technological knowledge that creates new demands - and the needs of nature,"

Nathan offers as a balanced view. "On balance, sometimes we make and do amazing things and sometimes we mess things up."

"Well, you're right, of course, Nathan," I agree. "We don't live in a bubble of idealism. The urges are constantly there to tear down and to create new things and to change the status quo."

The boys have been trading off driving all day today. It's time for me to let go of the status quo, take a turn at the wheel and carry us into the night. And it's going to be a long one. Almost 5:00 in the afternoon now means around 10:30 tonight to get to our destination in the Dakotas. We'll have a time change tomorrow when we leave the capitol of Pierre. The time-line follows the Missouri River from Pierre north and we will cross that imaginary line well after the sun rises as we go west. Central Time becomes Mountain Time, though the mountains don't start until we get close to Wyoming.

For now, we straddle the border between Nebraska and Iowa, as we follow Lewis and Clark north along the Missouri River. We have less than an hour before we cross into South Dakota.

"Hey, guys," I look over at them from the driver's perch, "we really let loose this morning with our creative animal noises and it was a day of learning a lot. What do you think of this? You both like Albert Einstein. In fact, I think, you both bear a resemblance to him. Yes you do!" I say when they give me doubtful looks. "Your hair flies wild in the wind, your faces are innocent of meanness and you have brains that come up with big surprises." I smile and I have their attention.

"Here's what Einstein says – and notice the present tense I'm using – 'says.' We do that with the sages, even when they're dead, because their words are still very much alive.

"The gift of fantasy has meant more to me than my talent for absorbing knowledge."

Nathan responded, "I don't disagree, but it doesn't quite strike me as my own opinion either. I love absorbing knowledge, and I love my talent for absorbing knowledge. But I believe I understand the connection here. Fantasy is what usually drives the talent for absorbing knowledge, and therefore drives learning itself. I am the epitome of that. The cosmos's vast nature, stretching to infinity and beyond compels me to discover as much as I can within my capability, and find how far the capability itself stretches."

Kenny has listened to every word, though his eyes are gazing at the green pastures, still rolling along. "I think fantasy and knowledge are close together in my head," Kenny offers. "A lot of things seem unreal to me. Am I making this up? This car, us and everything? This trip too? I have learned a lot mostly on my own, not in school. But what I know is what I make it be. I say that in my head. What I see I make up too. It's scary sometimes."

"Hmmm," I hum thoughtfully. "I think I understand what you're saying Kenny. We are all working to make sense of this world we're in. We're all kids learning how to do this thing called life."

Nathan projects again. "Yes, fantasy is actually vital for my learning. But here is where I'm developing my difference from Mr.

Onestone (ein means 'one' and stein means 'stone' in German). For me fantasy means getting knowledge, and using it. They are mutually inseparable notions. Obviously for most other people, it is different. For them, and you Kenny, the fantasy lies in the unknown, in the achievable-yet-far-away."

Yes, far away, I think, as I gaze out at the far horizon. So near and yet so far are we. Together in this van, but we are all alone in our minds. Far from our homes, unless your home is where your heart is, which for us right now is in the heartland of America.

"But, I not only see, hear and smell fantasy," Nathan continues with emphasis. "I taste it. I touch it. Ultimately I submerge myself in the ocean and fly up to those clouds to reach it. Or at least I try to."

Cumulus clouds fill the sky as I skirt Sioux City, Iowa. I cross the Missouri River again, this time east to west. Quickly Kenny spots the state sign. This is where the southeastern tip of South Dakota dips like a thumb into Iowa and Nebraska.

# CHAPTER 8

# SOUTH DAKOTA

The light is muted with cloud cover for our photo, as I pull off the highway. The big white rectangle, with a ribbon of green near the edge, reads South Dakota in red script. In the middle are the Mount Rushmore Presidential heads in gold. On the bottom is the phrase, GREAT FACES GREAT PLACES. The great faces of Kenny and Nathan smile, as they pose in front, and I snap their picture.

I get back in the driver's seat and we all settle in for a long haul. We made it to the Dakotas, to a place of great space, mostly flat or gently rolling, and few signs of civilization. The great faces are at the other end of this state, along with the Black Hills, a small mountain range leading to the Rockies. I like the feeling of flat emptiness as we roll along. And I love the accompanying quiet with no radio or CDs playing. We all seem to have agreed on this unless we vote unanimously for turning something on. We can hear ourselves think and talk. And Nathan starts talking about music.

"I've been watching some Disney movie clips at school on YouTube. Some have an original score of classical music and some have more contemporary music. It makes me realize how incredibly horrible normal modern music is with that stark comparison. Classical music, which is more or less the kind of music they had in every Disney movie until Tarzan, is the kind of music that evokes true emotions; it makes humans really and truly feel alive. But the more modern types of music, whether it be rock or pop or rap or indie or whatever names they have for the other genres, make me disgusted and horrified that this is where music is going. How did this happen?"

I can see that Nathan is on a rant, like I was with the Army Corps of Engineers a few hours ago. So I'm giving space to his strong feelings.

"The stretch from classical to ragtime to jazz was positive and creative. Those three kinds of music have merit to them, and they still evoke the human soul. But the more present one gets with music, the closer to caveman sounds one gets. I seriously equate these kinds of modern music with beating sticks on rocks, and with moaning, groaning and yelling. I don't understand how music has degraded and decomposed so badly. Does anybody have any insight into this? It really distresses me, with my only solace, and a fantastic one it is, being classical music."

Kenny, who does not like most classical music and reminded me of that on our North Carolina to Wisconsin leg of the trip, stays quiet, so I venture a response.

"I agree with you close to 100%, or as you might say more precisely, seventy-seven point seventy three percent. I'm glad you have such good taste in music! Classical music has been my love since I first was introduced to it at school in my youth. I was raised in a church with hymns that I sang and played on the piano, the viola and the French horn and I loved that too.

"Generally, I don't care for modern music as much as classical, but I have learned to appreciate a lot of it. I do like many of the modern composers, including Stravinsky, Mahler and Philip Glass. I've played Bartok and the French composers Debussy and Ravel on the piano and I still do and I love them. For listening, mostly I prefer classical music. As for how this modern music happened and do I have any insight into this, I don't have a good answer. It is all a process of creativity that evolves in ways that we might not all expect or appreciate. And then it will evolve some more to something perhaps more to our liking. And our tastes do change. I do think though, that some contemporary music expressions don't compare to the classical music of the eighteenth, nineteenth and twentieth centuries. So much skill and brilliance went into those compositions. Some modern music seems, by my figuring, to be created by chance and with a goofy notion, not by sweat and tears. How can you compare some of today's music with the beauty of Beethoven or Schubert?"

And with that, Nathan for the first time on this trip, took his headphones out of his bag, put a compact disc into the player, plugged the cord in and started listening to Beethoven's Ninth Symphony at top volume – we knew because a little of the sound was oozing away from the plugs in his ears.

Even at top volume, Beethoven would not have heard his own music. He was completely deaf at the time he composed the Ninth, an amazing achievement in itself, and 'listened' to it by beating time as he sat on the stage during its performance. Choral, as it is called, is the first of any symphonies that included a text that is sung (I've sung it) and was his last symphonic composition. This great German composer and virtuoso pianist completed it in 1824, three years before his death at age 57. The Ninth Symphony is thought by some to be the highest achievement of humankind, along with Shakespeare's Hamlet.

I see Nathan, with his intense enrapture with the music, and Kenny, seeming to be at peace with his thoughts and the world around him as he gazes out the window, and I think about their accomplishments over adversity. Kenny, with a shaky beginning socially and little drive to do anything, with professional and family concerns for him, has become a sweet friendly young man to everyone and is still finding his own way with his smarts and skills. He's not following any traditional path. Nathan, who lived alone in a world of his own creation as a toddler, who bore the psychic scars of being teased and taunted as an elementary school student, has persevered with his brilliance and plunged into our world with gusto. The marvel of it all makes me weep. What inimitable boys they are.

I manage to see, through my silent tears, some signs of civilization again as I exit I-29 north onto a bypass around Sioux Falls and head west on I-90. But the quiet prairie expanse quickly welcomes us again and the late light of spring is fast fading. I don't want my driver's attention to fade with it so I ask toward the mirror to Kenny in the seat behind me, "Kenny, may I rouse you out of your reverie? Will you please help keep me at full alertness? I don't want to be totally mesmerized by the quiet and the beams of my headlights."

"Yes, I'll do that," he eagerly offers. "I was just thinking about what's out there in the sky and I have an idea. Let's look for UFOs. We've done it before. I really want to see a UFO."

"Great idea!" I exclaim. "This is the perfect place to be. It's empty and flat. The horizon goes on forever in a full radius. There are no city lights. The skies have cleared enough to see more stars than you'll ever see in most places in the States. That's a waxing new moon," I say pointing to just above the horizon, "so, we don't have too much sky light. Any moving globes should stand out for us, especially if they have color. Another thing, many sightings are near military facilities. Ellsworth Air Force Base is almost directly west of us, at the foot of the Black Hills, but maybe not close enough to enhance our chances."

"I'm watching for anything moving or changing direction quickly," Kenny says, "but especially saucer shapes with rotating lights. And I would not mind being abducted, though I'd probably be really scared."

We do watch for the rest of the drive to Pierre. Nathan has finished listening to the over hour long Ninth Symphony and joins us in our search. Nathan and I have relatives and acquaintances, that have had impressive sightings of UFOs, but the mysterious spheres have eluded us. I have searched seriously for many years and only find other people who have seen them. Someday, maybe it will be my turn.

"My uncle and aunt saw a UFO when they were seven and eight years old," Nathan starts to tell us the story. "They lived on a military base and were walking by themselves in an adjacent neighborhood. They looked up and saw an object hovering over them about the height of a telephone pole, so it was close and huge. Other people saw it too and were running for cameras. The UFO was round and silver, with red, white and blue lights blinking on and off on a ring around the bottom half of the saucer shape. The top half moved the opposite direction from the bottom half. It was about 70 feet across. The noise it made was very quiet, like a low humming or vibrating sound. My eight-year old aunt had heard a lot from the adults about sightings in the news. Seeing this ship scared the heck out of her. She ran back home as fast as she could, dragging her brother with her. Many years later she was hypnotized to find out if she had been abducted. It was as she remembered it and she was relieved to find out that she had not been taken on board. Her brother, my uncle, has the same memory of it. My aunt married a military man who was on a Long Island beach when he saw a UFO come soaring out of the ocean into the air so fast and then it was gone. His description of the saucer was exactly the same as my aunt had remembered hers ten years earlier."

"I believe their story," Kenny says. "I think that many of the 'strange lights' that people have seen are probably alien craft."

"I believe their story and a lot of other stories I've heard or read," I say. "That's what they saw and believe. But I haven't had my own experience of it. What do you think now Nathan? I know your beliefs have been in flux."

"My father doesn't believe there is anything to it and that it is a total hoax. In fact he doesn't even believe his own brother and sister. This is the kind of position of many people, although it certainly has its merits as far as the desire for direct evidence, which seems to be fleeting. But it is at heart a position of 'denial' rather than skepticism. And as such, even my own scientist father is being very unscientific here. I personally strive to keep an open mind either way," Nathan answers. "I would like to study the technology of their amazing feats, and I know our government is keeping some information from the public. President Bill Clinton himself acknowledged the existence of Area 51. Before I form a real opinion, however, I want to collect more information and evidence.

"And as regards some of the controversy, I do worry for the U.S. Constitution. The signs they have posted on the perimeter of Area 51 say, more or less, 'If you enter here, you will have no rights and will be shot.' That's unconstitutional and anti-American. But my best course of action is to not focus on that now. I have a career to plan for."

None of us has detected any unusual feats of lights, speeding and shifting direction, in the sky and we are ready to call it a night.

I have turned off of I-90 for a short hop north to Pierre, in the exact geographic center of South Dakota. Earthly urban colored lights are appearing near the ground and we see a Super 8 Motel sign in yellow and red and black on West Sioux Avenue, homage again to the Native American Sioux, who still live here in the Dakotas. We check in and quickly collapse in our room. While Kenny soaks in the tub, Nathan reads his favorite book, the 725 page The Emperor of Japan: Meiji and His World, 1852-1912, by Donald Keene. A painting of the Meiji on the cover could be Nathan. The resemblance is uncanny. The boys have been courteously offering and taking turns carrying my laptop into motels and I will keep my brain in action and make some notes of the day, record keeper that I am. Then we can fade into the dark of the night. Tomorrow we see South Dakota's capitol.

The modest tan limestone capitol building that we see from the van has a plain flat facade, and is lined with row upon row of small rectangular windows. It sits on a flat green lawn, like everything else in this very small town of 12,000. The green copper dome barely rises above the fourth floor of windows. The structure is a modified version of the Montana state capitol in Helena, which we will be passing up. So this structure serves us as two capitol visits in one.

There is no one here except us. The parking lot, immediately in front of the capitol, sits empty under a cumulus cloud cover with light blue patches barely showing through. It is 8:00, early on a Saturday morning, and the doors are open, as they are every day of the year, a plebeian welcome for the common man.

But inside, our patrician sensibilities are treated with a surprising Greco-Roman architectural display in marble and glass. Victorian leaded glass channels outdoor light overhead in the dome as well as through a large arch of glass wrapped into an alcove of the ceiling called the Vault. At our feet are Terrazzo tiles, laid by Italian artisans, with their fifty-five legendary blue stones (although eleven more are missing), scattered throughout the capitol floors. Surrounding us are white marble walls and columns, each column lit near the top with four incandescent globes, all setting off the grand white-cloud marble staircase in a nouveau show of opulence.

Nathan makes a grand sweep up the marble steps and Kenny and I decide to take the elevator to catch up with him. When we reach the third floor and step into the rotunda and look up, there is Nathan on the top floor, leaning casually over the railing and calling down to us, "What took you so long?"

Kenny and I run up the last flight of the grand staircase to join Nathan for a quick round of the Senate and Legislative Galleries, but being a Saturday, nothing is in session. Republican Governor Mike Rounds is not in session either as we make our way past his office, down four flights of white-cloud marble, with murals of Greek goddesses overhead to symbolize the major interests in South Dakota livestock, industry and mining. We stop for a drink at one of the very tall (no need for the boys to bend over) ornate white marble water fountains found throughout the capitol. They resemble open seashells, more Greek symbolism, and this time in the form of water.

We still haven't seen a soul, when we exit to the parking lot and go back to our plain plebeian tan van.

We follow tree-lined streets through Pierre. This tranquil town was founded 125 years ago when the gold prospectors and the homesteaders transformed the Dakota Territory (now the two Dakota states) into the turbulent Great Dakota Boom. Through the years, the gold rush settled into steady mining, and the farmers and the cowboys prospered. The cowboys from the west corralled beef cattle and sheep, and the farmers from the east grew wheat, oats and hay, as they both still do today. The Missouri River, cutting through Pierre, also cuts the state diagonally in half.

With no towns on our westward route today, we don't expect to find any places for food. South Dakota is the 48th least populated state in the country (Wyoming where we're headed is the 50th). Most of the few towns in South Dakota collect on the eastern border along the Missouri River. Farms and ranches stretch over more than nine-tenths of the state and half the population lives on farms. So we give the meat and wheat industries a little support by heading to a Subway in Pierre and stocking up for the day. We are ready to again cross the river at the mid-point of its 2,341 mile-length.

We pass the exact spot where Lewis and Clark set up their tents, called Fort Pierre, along the Missouri River in September 1804. They recorded in their journals, with pen and India ink that the coyotes and wolves howled under the moonlight. The aggressive Teton Sioux were also a threat and the explorers stayed on guard for several sleepless nights. Chief Black Buffalo resolved the hostilities and the Corps proceeded on. As do we. Nathan gets us back onto Highway 83, going south this time and we leave 'city' life behind.

In the light of the sun, the prairie land stands out in broad relief. It's a flat, green canvas, ripe for a painter's brush. As in a Monet landscape, small puffy clouds float in and dot the green with shadows. The rolling shadowed spots mesmerize us with their surreal, dream-like beauty.

The silent land rolls on and on in sheets with barely a ripple of contour. There are virtually no cars on this four-lane highway and again as Nathan turns west onto I-90. One could go 200 miles an hour and hardly know it – there are few reference points to make sense to Einstein's formulas for speed of movement - no trees or hills whipping by. We also haven't seen a single police car on the highway since entering the state, so if there ever was a place to speed, this is it. We're all thinking it, I'm pretty certain, but we keep up our silence. And I let it happen. I suspected that our driver Nathan might be picking up speed and then I glanced surreptitiously from the seat behind him at the speedometer. The needle slowly veered right until it passed 100 miles per hour. It stayed there for a few seconds for us to capture the thrill and then it returned to a legal 75 mph. I said nothing. It was our group secret.

Breaking all the silence, I asked the boys, "Do you remember when you guys started to talk?"

"I was eight months old," Kenny said, "when I said my first

word. And just over a year when I started saying sentences. But I never talked to other kids. I was too shy and afraid."

"You were way ahead of me," Nathan added. "I remember deciding on purpose not to talk after my first year and until I was about two and a half. I was embarrassed to speak and it was easier not to. People were nice and talked with me and that was less complicated. The reason I started to talk was my brother. I remember him starting to make sounds that I thought might turn into words. I was scared of being beaten by him. So, I started to say my first words in complete sentences. My father remembers me when I was about three, talking to him about how, 'This is the way I see it,' with full linguistic ability."

When these boys were in their separate preschools fifteen years ago, they played by themselves. Kenny made believe he was a rabbit and he played with toys alone. Nathan paced the fringes of circle time, putting his fingers in his mouth as if pondering the universe. He didn't hear or notice instructions to sit or listen. In the classroom, neither one talked to the other children or to their teachers and if one talked it was to oneself. And now they converse freely with richness and smartness and fun. But we're quiet again. The landscape seems to ask for silence and for thinking about the past.

It is a good, rich, barren land here in the wild and wonderful upper-shelf states of the lower forty-eight. The Sioux Nation, made up of the rhyming and combining Dakota, Lakota and Nakota tribes, are part of the mix of cultures here, living in cities and scattered on nine Indian reservations in the state. They have had a tumultuous history of trying to save their land. The Sioux took over the land from other tribal groups that snatched the land from the Plains Villagers, a thousand years ago. The Plains Villagers claimed the land from the first known inhabitants of South Dakota, the Paleo-Indians who crossed the Bering Strait from Asia 10,000 years ago. This area has a long history of Indian Wars, between tribes and with the white man, to gain land and keep it. The Indian Wars ended with the Battle at Wounded Knee. Wounded Knee is just south of us and near the Nebraska border. The U.S. Cavalry massacred hundreds of Lakota Sioux - men, women and children - on a windswept hill, four nights after Christmas in 1890. The Army was perhaps avenging the death of Colonel George Custer fourteen years earlier in the Black Hills, at the lost Battle of Little Bighorn. A year before the Battle of Wounded Knee, North and South Dakota were created from the Dakota Territory, which in turn had been carved out of the original Louisiana Territory. Throughout the history of our bipedal race, the Indians and the white man were all displacing prior occupants of the land. Whoever is here first does not necessarily win out. The good land is in the hands of the white race now, as well as the Sioux, Latinos, Asians, African-Americans and Pacific Islanders, a rainbow of color right here in the Plains.

Nathan is passing up the road to Wounded Knee - we send our respectful thoughts - and is turning south toward the Badlands.

But the Badlands are far from bad. That word came from the Sioux who thought the landscape was eerie, and from the French because the land was hard to cross. In contrast, our highway takes us easily to a place that is a rare geological wonder.

Rising out of volcanic ash laid down 30 million years ago, like a phoenix, are spires, pinnacles, razor-edged ridges and steep canyons suddenly appearing in the late morning light. Who would have thought minutes ago, on the rolling grasslands that this otherworldly terrain was here? Who would have known that there are geological and paleontological secrets, buried in the sculpted rock, that are still being uncovered?

We park and walk over sandy soil of ash and lava to the cliffs. Walking, climbing, sitting, touching, looking, the boys and I take in the mystery. The action started 80 million years ago, when the Badlands were an inland sea. Over time, the land became uplifted. The layering of ash and soft sedimentary rock became eroded by wind and water, forming the landscape that we are seeing today. Rich fossil beds from 30 million years ago, in these 'bad' lands, have revealed the saber-toothed cat and ancestors of the camel named Poebrotherium and of the horse called Mesohippus. This is a prehistoric graveyard, but there is colorful life in the primrose and mariposa lily, that we find hidden in the rocks, and life force in the eagles we see flying overhead. Herds of bison, whose ancestors also lie under the millennia of rock, are grazing and roaming nearby on the prairie grassland. There are 40,000 bison in this state, in parks or on private land, half of all the herds in the U.S., and no longer endangered we are glad to know.

"We're ready to go," Kenny says. And we head back to the van and the highway that will take us to Wyoming and then to Montana. We'll stop at Mount Rushmore in the Black Hills later today. But first, we make a couple more stops along the road, winding through the eroded one-quarter million acres of the Badlands, and get out to view more of the grand sweep of gray and pink rock.

I saw that Nathan and Kenny had been enjoying the climb around the spires, but that they also seemed very contemplative sitting on the top of the mounds and staring into the distance. I could also tell that Nathan was bothered about something, by his silence and by the tense look on his face, and Kenny reflects this too. The joy of exploring seems to have dissipated.

"What are you thinking, guys?" I ask.

"Kenny and I were talking up on the top of the rocks," Nathan starts to unburden himself. "We agree that it is very nice and very pretty here, but it's windy and literally cold. I feel depressed about the white man destroying the Indians and their culture. They killed the Indians just to take over this land and what for? It's barren and useless and they massacred a people and a culture. I just feel sick."

Nathan is silently crying tears. I am feeling his distress and also feel such admiration for his beliefs and principles and his opening up his heart. My eyes are filling with tears with the thought of it all. Kenny is sensitively silent, looking with understanding and caring at his buddy.

"Nathan," I venture, "you're as brave as the Indians to show your feelings. At Wounded Knee the white men did kill a band of Native families. The Sioux were here before us and they were fleeing and not even fighting back when the soldiers attacked them with their guns. It was horribly violent, unfair and a sad chapter in our history. But we can't undo it now. We can do what we can to keep justice alive in our own lives and those around us."

"I know," Nathan said in a calmer voice. "And that's what I do and want to do in my life – work for justice. Wherever my career takes me."

Now, I know that both these boys have had their own pains and hurts to deal with. Nathan in his early years was taunted and rejected by his peers, and admonished harshly and dismissed as a tragedy by professionals. When he started taking the bus to school in kindergarten, the other kids on the bus teased him mercilessly. They would say, "You're odd." "Why do you stick your fingers in your mouth?" "We could punch you." They called out these kinds of taunts endlessly. He sat alone on the bus, if he could manage it, to try to separate himself from the verbal assault. He has had an early and harsh dose of the cruelty in the world. Kenny felt badly as a kid that he didn't fit in. He says that the kids did not tease him but that they saw him as odd. He still feels badly that he still doesn't fit in. He wishes that things were different. Both Nathan and Kenny are ripe for feeling the pain of others.

But, our souls are soothed with the beauty of the rock and the ride west. In less than two hours we are at the border where South Dakota meets Wyoming.

# CHAPTER 9

# WYOMING

WYOMING WELCOMES YOU, says the state sign. It shows a high mound of rock with gold ridges and a silhouette of a bucking horse and a cowboy. He's hanging on with his right hand, and with his left hand he's holding, with flair, a cowboy hat high in the air. Yee Ha! We're in Wyoming!

The boys look ever so confident and endearing as they lean casually and comfortably against their posts, making short shadows toward me as I take a snapshot of their efflorescing lives.

We are going to Devil's Tower, the rock on that sign, to see a 40 million year old monolith. One of Nathan's college friends, a native of Wyoming, had urged him to see it and so we are.

The elevation of the surrounding prairie is rising to 4,000 feet. We are in a state of grasslands and mountains. Far to the west near the Wyoming-Idaho border, beyond our travel route, is the blue and jagged Grand Teton Mountain Range. Among those mountains, thrusting almost 14,000 feet into the thin, clear air, live the moose and bison. The Rocky Mountains begin there. Just north of the Tetons are two million acres of Yellowstone, home to the black and grizzly bears, and filled with thousands of thermal vents. Deep down to its molten-rock core, the restless earth is rumbling and fuming steam from its fumeroles and bubbling mud pots, to its geysers and natural hot springs. Seeing those geological wonders would mean at least half a day's drive and back again, each way, through the Bighorn Mountains and we don't have time for that this time. And the Oregon Trail, crossing southern Wyoming, is not an option. The Trail served the settlers well – the homesteaders, fur traders and gold prospectors, the Mormons congregating at Salt Lake and the cowboys-to-be - all looking for free land, compliments of the U.S. government and to the detriment of the Indians, in the far west. Then the Union Pacific Railroad was built in Wyoming. It connected westward with the Central Pacific Railroad building eastward. This first transcontinental railroad, stretching from Council Bluffs, Iowa, to Sacramento, California, was completed in 1869. It usurped the need for a wagon and oxcart path. So we three modern day travelers in an 'iron conveyance' stay course on the middle plane.

Directly south of us to the Colorado border, another half day's drive that we will not make, is Cheyenne, population 50,000, the Wyoming capital and the largest city in this sparse state of the fewest people in the country.

"I'll tell my friend," Nathan says, "that we did not have time to visit the capitol with its real gold leaf dome."

"And as for the Governor," I add, "Democratic Governor Dave Freudenthal, the common man, is listed in the phone book, so we can give him a call if we want to, rather than an attempted visit."

"Maybe I will phone him," Nathan kids. "I may want his permission to prospect for gold. Kenny, you could prospect with me.

Mineral extraction, especially coal, is the main industry in Wyoming, but there is still gold to be found."

"I'd like to do that. It suits me. I like to be outdoors, I like to take chances and I might make some money like I hope to do with playing poker," Kenny says enthusiastically. He takes it seriously.

"Mmmm," I pondered out loud. "The poor man's coal and the rich man's gold. Gambling can incur both. But, if you do plan to dredge, you need a state permit and I wish you luck. One of my brothers, a chemical engineer, prospected for gold and uranium and other minerals for many years in his free time in this very state. What he was left with was thousands of dollars down the drain."

"Or dribbled through the gold sifter," Nathan jokes.

We turn off of I-90 onto U.S.14, skimming the fringes of Wyoming's Black Hill Country, home to the Black Hills Spruce and ponderosa pine. The Black Hills extend from here back into South Dakota, where we'll visit again later today. Triceratops made these Hills their home 65 million years ago.

Kenny, Nathan and I can see, from miles away, a fluted, flat-topped cone that rises hundreds of feet into the air. Now, stepping out of the van onto its rocky floor, we see the impressive sight up close. Alone in profile against the deep blue sky is another mystery like the Badlands. Where did this come from in the middle of the plains? How do you explain such eerie beauty? The Indians considered this as holy, the site of the ancient Sun Dance, but called it Bad God's Tower. Today it's called Devil's Tower National Monument. It is likely they were trying to frighten off the explorers, but without success. Tribes living in what is now Wyoming - the Shoshones and the Arapahos, the Lakota, Crows, Cheyenne, Bannocks, Blackfoot and Northern Ute - all ranged here centuries ago. Only remnants of tribes have survived. The Europeans, our descendants, arrived in the eastern United States 500 years ago, but it took awhile for them to get to Wyoming. John Colter is the earliest known white explorer, because he told stories about it, that were passed on 200 years ago. He was part of the Lewis and Clark expedition, following the Missouri River in Montana. John left the expedition on their return trip from the Pacific, to scout what we now call the Grand Tetons and Yellowstone. His tales sparked the beginning of the influx of explorers and homesteaders to the West.

Much more recently, Devil's Tower became the focus of the movie, Close Encounters of the Third Kind, about more technologically advanced 'explorers' arriving, not in covered wagons, but in spinning UFOs.

Geologists say that this huge knuckle of rock in front of us was created with a flow of molten magma 60 million years ago, pushing its way up into a layer of sedimentary rock. It cooled and shrank and separated into flutes or columns. The exposed volcanic mass eroded through centuries of wind, rain and snow into today's knob of a monolith. We're looking at the core of an ancient volcano, made of a rock called phonolite that is iron-rich red and glistening in the bright sunlight.

In contrast, the Sioux creation story tells of seven girls being attacked by a giant bear. They crowd onto a small rock and pray to the stone gods to save them. The gods cause the rock to grow higher and higher until the girls are out of reach. The bear continues to claw for the girls, though, causing the striations in the rock. The girls meanwhile, escape to the sky to become the sisters in the constellation of Pleiades.

Though no bear is chasing Nathan and Kenny, they quickly scramble up and over the rocks. They exude energy and joy and I catch it too as I climb the path. Nathan is partway up the rocky base ahead of Kenny, and I collect some snow from below the rocks. I expertly make a snowball – some childhood skills are not lost – and throw it to Kenny, higher up the slope. He catches it and throws it on the top his head gleefully. He makes his own snowball and tosses it to me and another one that he throws high into the air. Then he runs up the trail to catch up with Nathan who is continuing to clamber over the rocks.

"Hey, look at the climbers!" Nathan calls down to me and he points up to the cliff.

Sure enough, there are several tiny figures on the nearly vertical walls. They are testing their skills, with ropes and pulleys, helmeted and climbing along the vertical channels to reach the top. They belay each other - securing themselves at the end of a rope - with rappel devices, descenders and harnesses attached to the sturdy belts around their waists. More than a thousand brave souls a year climb almost 900 feet from the rocky base to the flat summit of sagebrush and grass. They each look like a fly on the wall.

"They're calling to each other," Nathan calls again, "in climbing lingo."

And then I too notice the distant calls.

The climbers, Nathan and Kenny, make it up the rocky slope to the bottom of the wall. Looks are deceiving. It is so much further than it looks. What must climbing the wall be like?! When the boys decide to turn around, I do too, from halfway up the path.

"You guys got a good workout and I did too. It felt great," I say. "And the day couldn't be more beautiful."

"Yes, yes," they answer, as we all approach the van and hop in. "That was cool, nice, interesting, pleasant and scary," Nathan says. "It's time to go to Montana."

Montana is just a short hop across the border on Highway 112, and then it will be a short stay for us.

"This will be my 35th state," Nathan says with pleasure. "Being in as many states as possible is my biggest reason for making this trip."

"It will be my 17th state," Kenny calculates.

"Montana has strong similarities to Wyoming, and you've probably realized it too," I say to the boys. "They share the Rocky Mountains, shaped by glaciers, in the west. They both have plains in the east, outside our windows, the domain of the Plains Indians centuries ago. Mining for minerals and gems is a big industry in both states. And cattle grazing and skiing and touring. Put us in that last category. As for skiing, I haven't skied in these western states but I've skied in Switzerland. Does that count?"

"Not really. Montana is on top of the U.S." Nathan says. "It borders three provinces of Canada - British Columbia, Alberta and Saskatchewan. I remember that from before I started kindergarten. Montana is a wide state and geographically is the fourth biggest state in the United States. Tomorrow we'll be east of here in Canada's province of Manitoba."

"Hey, guys, if we could do an Evil Knievel jump west to Idaho, we could cover more territory. He jumped the Snake River Canyon in Idaho in a rocket-powered skycycle. Montana claims him as a resident for all of his growing-up years. There's another fantasy idea for you, Kenny!"

"I have a car, but I'd like to get a motorcycle in the future instead of a car," Kenny admits. "I like to drive fast. I'd like to do daredevil tricks. Doing things on my own that are almost dangerous is fun. Pushing myself to the limits of what I'm capable of."

# CHAPTER 10

# MONTANA

Kenny is driving us across the state border, no risks here, into Carter County at the southeastern corner of Montana.

"Photo-op time guys," I say as I spot the state sign on the right side of the road.

Kenny pulls over and we all leap out. The sun is bright in the big blue Montana sky and casting shadows almost the length of the boys. They have switched sides for the first time and are standing like sentinels at their new posts. Their outside arms are wrapped around the wooden beams, their hands reaching for their chests, as if holding flags. They seem happy with the world, smiling toward me. The wide rectangular sign high above them is a jigsaw cutout of the shape of the state. MONTANA stands out in red against a yellow sun, with an eyebrow of white cloud at the top of the circle. 'Welcome to' is written in red against a background of blue.

This sweeping land is ranching country. From here, it seems empty of people, buildings and even animals. Above us and around us is the big blue sky that Montana is famous for. The heavens seem endless. "It looks like someone has abandoned this state or never lived here in the first place," I observe. "We have it to ourselves. I know that the antlered creatures of this state outnumber the people."

In fact Montana has less than one million in population and way more deer and antelopes than people. All of Carter County in the bottom-right corner of the state, where we are right now, has only 1,300 residents, the size of my small childhood hometown. Adjacent to Carter County is Custer County, where the Sioux killed Colonel Custer, leading the 7th Cavalry of the U.S. Army. Crazy Horse, an Oglala-Lakota Sioux, led the Sioux forces, in 1876, in the Battle of Little Bighorn. Six counties west of us rises Lewis and Clark County, home to the capital city of Helena. A copper dome tops the State Capitol, though gold rush riches built the town. Besides being the fourth biggest state, Montana ranks another fourth, for the U.S. production of copper. Nearby, in Three Forks, is a river canyon that Lewis called 'the gates of the rocky mountains,' when he recorded it on July 19, 1805, exactly two hundred years and two months and five days before our trio's arrival today in Montana. His Corps of Discovery found three rivers there, forking out of the headwaters of the Missouri River that we have been flirting with ever since we entered the state of Missouri.

"Helena, Montana!" Nathan calls, getting our attention, and tells us his own short story from the backseat of the van, "now capital of this fine state. Billings and Butte, the birthday brothers, born at the same time, fought each other. But being equally strong, they both lost. So Helena came and stole the territory."

"That's about it," I assent with a chuckle. "It was a hot contest between towns throughout the Louisiana Territory (purchased by

President Thomas Jefferson from the French and then divided into smaller territories). First to be the territorial capital and then to be the capital of the state when they reached statehood."

Butte and Billings, like brothers, share a close longitude coordinate – 112.941 and 108.5, with the Missouri headwaters between them. They were born at the same time as other boomtowns in Montana in the late 1800s. With the discovery of silver, gold and copper, towns erupted out of sterility. By 1888, Helena had fifty millionaires. Billings, the county seat of Yellowstone County, and just north of Yellowstone Park in Wyoming, was founded as a railroad town in 1882. Frederick H. Billings, a resident of Helena, was president of the Northern Pacific Railroad, which was vital to the success of the mineral boom. And Butte, in Silver Bow County, along with Custer County, is where the Battle of Little Bighorn was fought. It was established as a mining town in the 1880s.

"Guys," I continue while looking at the sparse landscape, "Butte, besides being a copper boomtown, was home to the saloons - our romantic notion of the life force of the Wild West. And Butte gave birth to the red light district, there being a lack of women in the bursting population of explorers and settlers."

Both Kenny and Nathan laugh. "Where are the women now?" Kenny asks. "I don't see them."

"Well, I don't see a sign of a woman or a man here," I observe. "Give me a booming mineral rich town full of men looking for women, but magically transported from the 19th century to the 21st century.

On second thought, NO, don't give me that. The men then were too rough on the edges."

Calm and quiet single-lane Highway 112 has become Alzada Road, leading we hope to some sign of civilization. A small short box of a building, with an RV parked behind, has appeared on our right. The sign reads B & J's Convenience Store, Alzada, Montana. So this is a town. We are virtually alone in God's country, spread to the limits of vision and beyond. It is good to get out and stretch in this open expanse of land. Then we enter B & J's to take a look around.

The boys and I are warm, friendly customers, though we're not expecting or planning to buy food. We have plenty in the van. But the place where we least expected to find food actually has an abundance of offerings on their menu. Is it the isolation that brings out the hospitality of the rare store that does exist? Baskets of crispy potatoes and salmon – no oceans here so where did this come from? Mountain streams? Chili and drummies, french fries and sandwiches and more, and we pass it all up. But sarsaparilla catches the boys' eyes. Even though they have sworn off soda the last couple of days, they buy the brown liquid showing in an attractive glass bottle with a picture of a cowboy painted on. Then we say thank you very much to the one person – the clerk - whom we have seen and met in Montana and we are back in the van.

Goodbye Montana! We leave you behind, almost before we began. We start out on a new southeastern path, Highway 212, cutting off the northeastern corner of Wyoming, to return to South Dakota.

# CHAPTER 11

# MOUNT RUSHMORE

South Dakota, here we are again, passing up your sign this time. Two hours driving will take us to Mount Rushmore in the Black Hills.

"Hey, Kenny and Nathan," I casually say. "What about all those girls that you didn't see and never met in Montana? Would you wish there were some around?"

I dare to bring up girls in our conversation, because I understand where both Kenny and Nathan are at, with their feelings and experiences (or lack of them) with the female population. However, I realize there is a lot that I don't know about what goes on in their heads.

"Of course. I would enjoy having them around," Nathan responds. "It's the same old thing. I wish I had a girlfriend and I don't. And it's not for lack of trying. Women do like me and I get along well with them. But when I ask them out, they say no because they're too busy or for other reasons, or I say no to them because I learn quickly about people and I can tell if they are not right for me. Most important for me is that they have a love of learning like I do. I haven't found many people who really care about learning in the huge way that I do."

"I want a girlfriend, too," Kenny speaks up. "But it hasn't

worked out for me. I'm too shy to ask girls out."

"What happened to the girl that you sent flowers to?" I ask Kenny. "That was such a sweet thing to do."

"I didn't hear from her, maybe because I went to Spain right afterward. I did see her in the halls in school in the Fall, but we didn't talk. After we graduated we did several things together but it didn't really lead anywhere."

Now, I know from what Nathan has said, that Kenny is passive about almost anything that has to do with girls, and he rarely makes a step to get their attention. He has desires but doesn't have the action.

I feel for these boys. Like all first timers, they try, flounder and learn, and hopefully don't get too discouraged or cynical. But the urges are strong for 19-year-old boys, and they want girlfriends so badly. Both Nathan and Kenny have such positive qualities that you would want everyone to be open to and embrace. But there might be just one thing or more about them that some girl does not like.

Both boys have admitted to falling in love with several girls from middle school, high school and now college The boys have made efforts to show their interest, with email, instant messaging and in person. Nathan has had experience with making overtures to a girl he liked, and then finding out that her boyfriend was angry at him. Nathan didn't know that the girl had a boyfriend and it hurt him to the point of tears. He had misread signals and social cues, and then had to endure angry words. It's a tough world out there.

"Kenny," I say. "You are a good looking young man and smart and very likeable. You are very nice to be with. You'll find the right one some day."

"You need to find a career to support yourself, though," Nathan admonishes. "Girls don't like slackers."

"Kenny, I agree with Nathan. It's important in life to be able to support yourself."

"The girls I would want to go out with, wouldn't care that I don't have money," Kenny offers.

I could see that Nathan was feeling distress, by the look on his face, as he spoke again. "Having a girl's boyfriend get angry with me when I didn't know she had a boyfriend was horrible and miserable," Nathan admits, with a catch in his throat.

"I'm so sorry, Nathan," I say with feeling in my words and tears in my eyes.

"And unrequited love," Nathan offers, "is one cause of my bouts with heartburn. It's a nasty feeling. I have been feeling bothered this whole trip because of my lack of a girlfriend."

"I so wish I could help you feel better," I sympathize. "I didn't know that was nagging at you this whole time. But, good for you for being so honest about your feelings. If it helps, know that you are a wonderful person with so many amazing qualities. Any girl that sees that and appreciates it, has good fortune to be with you."

"Yes. Thank you." he sweetly responds.

"You're welcome. And you know what? Both of you have had

some rough patches, but you are really trying to do the right things to get what you want. Keep putting yourselves out there, learn to enjoy the process, and eventually you will find your match.

"Sometimes our view of ourselves gets distorted with what other people may think about us and sometimes we can learn from what others think about us. But it's important to keep feeling good about ourselves. People you want in your life will be generally attracted to that feeling of goodness."

We are all silent for a while, staring out at the ascending hills. Then I add, "Look at the slanting, sparkling sunlight on the Black Hills around us. We're immersed in earthly beauty.  Can you feel mother nature's warm caress?"

The conversation ends. Goodness fills the air, replacing the sadness we all felt. There is comfort in the slopes of dense evergreen. We've entered and are looping through a granite mountain range, rising out of the sea of green prairie to our backs.

The tallest peaks in the United States, east of the Rockies, are here. From these hills, eighteen of them rise to over 7,000 feet.

Nathan informs us that the tallest peaks east of the Black Hills are the Black Mountains from the boys' native North Carolina. The tallest of them is Mount Mitchell at 6,684 feet.

We're driving now right near Harney Peak, the highest one of all in these Hills, at 7,242 feet. A geologic uplift created it, as well as all of the Black Hills, the Badlands and Devil's Tower, about 40 - 60 million years ago. Spires and pinnacles of rock surprise us, as they thrust out of the rich, dark green, luxuriant stands of spruce, mahogany, juniper and ponderosa pine. Vast cave mazes are below us, in the cracks left by the upward thrust of molten rock.

There's gold and silver in them thar hills, too, and wooly mammoth fossil beds, precursor of the elephants we saw in the Omaha zoo. The mammoths were buried in the rock, when they became extinct about 10,000 years ago, near the end of the ice age. And there are ghost towns and Indian claims to the land – spiritual claims and squatting rights for the sacred and the solid ground. The Hills are chock-full of things we do not even see.

We could climb without ropes or drive to the barren summit of Harney Peak, with an old fire lookout and a spectacular view at the top. The whole range of mountains would spread out around us, appearing from that distance as black as in Paha Sapa, the name given by the Sioux to the Black Hills.

Oh Great Spirit, whose voice I hear in the winds, and whose breath gives life to all the world . . . let me walk in beauty, and make my eyes ever behold the red and purple sunset, Lakota Chief Yellow Lark prayed in 1887.

With the sun lowering in the sky, we pass up the big climb and wind our way through the hills to see four presidents, enshrined in a granite mountain face.

Mount Rushmore is 5,725 feet high and we have arrived at the museum below. Eager to see what we came for, we pass up the exhibits and walk up the ramp to the terrace. There it is directly in front of us, a grand view, in the shadows of the early evening light of mid-May. We see a broad wall of exposed granite. It faces southeast to catch most of the days' light, helping the workers to carve and sculpt the rock three-quarters of a century ago and for the viewers to see today. The presidential heads are nested into a curve of rock.

George Washington, our first president, is first on the left, and the most prominent of the four. His collar, as Commander of the Continental Army, and his left shoulder are carved out of the rock. Just the heads were carved of the three remaining presidents. Thomas Jefferson, our third president, is next to Washington and set back slightly. Theodore Roosevelt, the 26th president is further back and facing east. Abraham Lincoln, our 16th president, is on the far right and spaced apart to accommodate his different angle.

Gutzon Borglum was the designer and sculptor, and he picked this site himself. He also chose the presidents he thought should be memorialized, though Calvin Coolidge, the Republican President at the time, also had a say. Coolidge insisted that two Republicans be chosen to balance out Washington and Jefferson. President Washington did not want any political party affiliation, though some historians call him a Federalist. President Jefferson founded the Democratic-Republican Party, and Democrats like to claim him as the originator of their party and their ideals. Presidents Lincoln and Theodore Roosevelt were both Republican. Work started in 1927, with the chosen four representing our country's first 150 years. Nathan, our aficionado of Presidents, says that, regardless of the method for choosing, these four presidents were the best choices, outstanding for their accomplishments and for the moral compasses by which they lived. Ethical men they were.

Washington led our nation from its colonial beginnings to become a united republic. Jefferson was author of the Declaration of Independence, a grand statement of our philosophy as a nation, and he was the mastermind of the Louisiana Purchase. Theodore Roosevelt was a champion of natural resources and built the Panama Canal that opened our nation to the whole world. Lincoln restored the Union and ended slavery. All were landmark events in our nation's history carried out by courageous, forward-thinking, principled Presidents.

"Nathan, should I even open up the subject of the quality of these men versus what followed?" I venture. "It's so hard to stomach the foibles and mismanagement and misuse of office of some of our later Presidents."

"I don't want to think about that right now," he answers. "I just want to think about these Presidents."

Nathan has the capability of expounding for days about these men. His historical knowledge is vast and he can retrieve it in an instant. He loves the Presidents with a passion beyond that of anyone else I have known. This intense interest started as a toddler and it is manifest today. He searches for and absorbs information in books and at historic sites, from teachers and wherever he can learn and see more.

For now, we gaze quietly at these men. We descend and climb the open amphitheater steps. The flags of every state in the union are hanging at the top of high metal posts, lined up along the outside rim of the curved bleachers. Flags of states that we are adding daily to our lists of 'what states I have been to,' are flying freely in the breeze. We walk the paths closer to the heads. The boys run and climb. Kenny is lithe as an arboreal monkey, jumping and leaping off of concrete steps and ledges and off of the rocks. Nathan leaps too and takes long strides up and around the paths and below the carvings above.

The carvings originated with models in clay. The artist Borglum looked at masks, paintings and photographs to make his models. Plaster casts were made from the models and some of the casts were displayed on the mountain in the 1920s as a guide for the artisans. The models were sized to be a ratio of one inch on the model to one foot on the mountain. A 'pointing machine,' making three separate measurements, helped determine degrees and angles of the three-dimensional head. Then the removal of stone began. Pneumatic drills, chisels, hammers and wedges, and dynamite were all used to blast away almost a half million tons of Mount Rushmore's granite. Slowly the faces emerged, 60 feet from chin to top. The sculptor Borglum died the year it was finished in 1941, fourteen years after it was started.

Now we're ready in the lowering light to enter the sculptor's studio. There are models of the heads and carving tools on display.

Nathan is especially impressed with the drawings of the full size models that the Presidential men were intended to be.

"It's unfinished," he said. "The sculptures should have been completed. The original plan was that the figures would be carved from head to waist and they did not do it. That bothers me a lot. Why didn't they do what was in the plan?"

"They ran out of money for one thing," I say. "Almost one million dollars of federal money was enough to spend. And the public lost interest in continuing the work. So it died along with Borglum."

I'm sure that Nathan had some idea, before I said it, of why they shut down the project, but he can be adamant about his beliefs. He likes a sense of completion, about seeing and ticking off all the states and about the Presidents in stone. The intention was not fulfilled. The work was not completed. He is pure and consistent about what he thinks should be and he says it. And you have to respect him for that.

"Are you ready to go, guys?" I ask.

We leave the presidents behind and wind our way in the van to another granite monument, a few minutes away. Nathan pulls off the road and we see Crazy Horse in the darkening sky. This Oglala-Lakota Sioux warrior helped defeat Custer and the U.S. Cavalry, in that famous Battle of Little Bighorn, back in Custer County, in Montana. The head of Crazy Horse shows in sharp profile on the top of Thunderbird Mountain. The horse he will sit astride is yet to come. It's a sculpture-in-progress, wanting more funds, and hoping to become the largest sculpture in the world.

"This is unfinished too," Nathan says. "It's half way between sculpture and nature. At Mount Rushmore and here, they first destroyed the mountain and then they didn't finish the artwork. It's depressing. And I think Custer deserved what he got."

"I don't like to see the mountain destroyed any more than it is," I say. "I wish we had let nature be at Mount Rushmore and at this mountain. But this is retribution for the Indians who gave up their land for the Presidents. If they complete the sculpture, it will carve into a lot more of that beautiful mountaintop. Enough is enough and I've seen enough. I'm ready to move on. How about you guys?"

Within a half hours' drive we arrive in Rapid City, on the eastern edge of the Black Hills and the western edge of the Plains. It is the biggest city around these remote, unpopulated parts, after Sioux Falls, on the eastern end of South Dakota. Rapid City, population 62,167 and elevation 3,202 feet, was incorporated in 1882. The discovery of gold by the Custer Expedition in the Black Hills gave birth to this town, though most gold mining has ceased today. It's named after the spring-fed Rapid Creek that flows close by, as we get out of the van at the Howard Johnson motel.

It is dark and we are ready for a good night's sleep. We've passed up Rapid Creek, but an indoor pool awaits us. We all submerge in the water as in an amorphous liquid. The boys do laps and then collapse with pleasure in the hot tub, while I do my exercises in the pool, and then suspend my body in the water and suspend my mind in time.

Isak Dineson, the novelist, once said, "The cure for anything is salt water - sweat, tears, or the sea." The day is over and we have done climbs and laps and exercises, with a salty, watery residue left clinging to our skin. We have shed our salty tears over injustice to the Indians and the boys' sadness with girls. The inland sea that covered the Northern Plains 80 million years ago is long gone, but a spring-fed creek is near us. And now we are each immersed in a pool of water filled with rich chloride salts. We are healing.

As we head to our room, and remembering Nathan's breaking the 3-digit speed barrier, earlier today, I quietly say for Nathan's ears only, "You have bragging rights now, Nathan."

"Yes I know," he said. "I'm glad I did it."

The morning comes quickly, and after the breakfast buffet, I pay the bill. At the end of the trip, we will split all gas and motel costs three ways. We are a democratic group. No age or gender discrimination here. And an altruistic trio we are. Each of us wanting happiness and good health for all.

# CHAPTER 12

# CROSSING SOUTH DAKOTA EAST

This is Sunday, May 15th, 'Day 5' for the three of us. The sun is out and the highway rolls out ahead of us. "We're driving all the way across South Dakota today!" Nathan exalts. "And north to North Dakota and across the border to Ca-na-da."

"No particular sights to see," I add. "Just a lot of driving."

The boys make a quick run into Arby's for grilled chicken fillet sandwiches to eat later in the van. "They call it natural chicken," Nathan laughs and projects his voice in an un-natural way. "Arby's Chicken Naturals is made with 100% all-natural chicken. Our chicken starts in its most natural form – not poked, prodded or altered in any way which leaves you with chicken that – get this – is all chicken. As opposed to the chicken you might find at other quick service restaurants, which tends to get injected with stuff like salt, water or phosphates. That's exactly what you won't find at Arby's. Experience chicken that truly tastes like chicken."

All three of us laugh at his quoting of the sales pitch and Kenny adds in his soft and playfully mischievous voice, "Well, we will enjoy this chicken, cluck, cluck, cluck."

"Thank goodness," Nathan exclaims, "chickens are so low on the intelligence scale that I am willing to eat them. You know a chicken brain is the size of a peanut. And Arby's says they are not abused. But, they're definitely factory farmed and that's abuse."

Kenny gets us onto I-90 east for a long, straight shot to Sioux Falls, South Dakota, where Iowa, Minnesota and South Dakota intersect. Then we will head north.

Just past Rapid City, I lean forward to tell Kenny, "Just north of us, is Ellsworth Air Force Base. Remember the search for UFOs the other night? I don't see any air activity happening right now, UFOs or man-made. The B1 Bomber is the only aircraft flown out of Ellsworth.

"Is it a big plane?" Kenny asks.

"I don't know, but it's supersonic. Nathan's Uncle Jim was in the Air Force for many years and flew C-130s, a cargo plane. He would know. C-130s are a big plane to fit tanks and Lord knows what else. But we know the B1-Bomber is fast. What is the speed of sound?"

"Through air, it's about 1280 kilometers per hour," Nathan says as he looks over from his reverie in the front passenger seat.

"What's that in miles?" I ask, not expecting his 'at the ready' metric system.

"770 miles per hour,"

"Let's say," I suggest, "that it flies 900 mph. The map shows, using my pinkie-finger middle bone as a measure, the distance across South Dakota from Rapid City to Sioux Falls to be about 340 miles. That means it would take the plane less than a half hour. What's the math?"

Nathan calculates out loud, 340 miles divided by 900 mph,

and concludes, "It would take .377 hours or 22.62 minutes for the B1-Bomber. For us, divide 340 miles by 75 mph, and it will take 4.4 hours. Bomber wins, wings down."

"Well it is called a swing-wing aircraft," I inform. "Whatever that means."

I think Kenny was inspired with the thought of the plane's speed. He told me months ago, that he once drove over 100 mph. So the quiet South Dakota Interstate Highway System was just waiting for him to do it again, as Nathan did yesterday. I hardly noticed, but found out later that Kenny had indeed broken the three-digit barrier. But we all knew this was an exception to their normal driving. They have been very good this whole trip to stay close to the speed limit. I spoke with them early in our travels about keeping the safety of everyone in mind. I expect they will continue to drive safely the rest of the trip, but I understand their wanting to break that forbidden barrier once in their lives. Well, twice for Kenny.

"I want to build and fly a plane," Nathan says with a yearning in his voice. "I might study aeronautical and astronautical engineering after college to get the knowledge to be able to do it."

"Where would you fly to?" Kenny wonders.

"Around the world. And I might use it for business. I'm thinking of a lot of possibilities for a career. Being able to fly would be useful in a lot of professions."

"I would like to be able to fly planes, too," Kenny admits. "But I would do it for the fun of it."

"It would cost money," I warn. "Are you guys prepared to spends thousands of dollars on a plane plus all the costs of upkeep and airport costs?"

"I would build the plane," Nathan says again. "That would make it cheaper. Plus, I might make enough money."

"Can I ride with you, if I don't have enough money?" asks Kenny, impishly. Nathan answers with a slightly disapproving frown that moves to a grin under the surface.

With money as a segue, I change the subject. "Nathan, way back in Independence, you were talking about all the people who don't have enough money for health care. Your favorite guy Truman was sympathetic to people needing to have their health needs met. But early on as President he did not support universal health insurance."

"But then he did," Nathan says. "He was inspired by former President Franklin D. Roosevelt. President Truman stated that of all our national resources, none is of more basic value than the health of our people."

"But Congress and the people did not support it," I counter. "And Truman lived in simpler times. It was hard to anticipate the boondoggle it might become way down the road. The Democrats have wanted universal health care for years. That means the government foots the bill. What do you want?"

"Yes, if it were done during Truman's time, we would not have any trouble now. I feel that health care is a human right, and so the government should pay for it," he responds.

"You have a point about if it were done in Truman's time, then not having any trouble now. But the government is us," I say back. "That means that we all are paying for someone who has not managed their money well enough or saved enough for a rainy day."

"If I have a broken leg, or cancer, or a disease, I want to be treated with no worries about time or money."

"That would be nice, but do you know what is happening in countries with universal health care, like Sweden, where I have visited disillusioned relatives, or Canada? They are scaling back because it is emptying the coffers of government. And people in Canada come here to be able to get quicker, better care and they pay for it. Our system has thrived on free enterprise and competition, mixed with government money for medical research."

"Insurance companies are pure evil," Nathan intones. "They should not dictate who lives or dies."

"Insurance companies are using good business sense, as you will do as a businessman, if you become one in any enterprise. They meet peoples' health needs, while making a profit. It's a system that has worked well, though there may be some flaws and kinks. Having the government run another massive entitlement program like social security, whose coffers are dry, will put us further into debt. Plus it encourages the mentality of dependence. I don't need to take care of it because someone else will, kind of thinking."

"The basic fact," Nathan returned, "is that people shouldn't use insurance in the first place. It's almost certainly a waste of money. People should save instead. I care about people getting the health care they need."

"Nathan, you can have compassion for people and do what you want to or don't want to do, personally, to aid in their needs. It's a free country. But, the government isn't the repository of compassion. Having the government pay for someone's health care gets us all off the hook – me from showing compassion in my own way, and the person hooked on the system from taking responsibility for themselves."

"You've been pretty quiet, Kenny. Do you have any thoughts on this?"

"I think I'm in the middle. I see what Ethel is saying about the cost to government, and I understand Nathan's wanting to have everyone get what they need."

"I'm feeling a pain in my stomach right now," Nathan blurts out. "Maybe we'll have to stop at an emergency room."

"I hope not," I say and I'm hoping he's saying that at least partly in jest. He does have a stomach-acid problem, after all. "But, be glad Nathan, that you have your parents' hard-earned health insurance."

"Which keeps on being revoked because people move around to new jobs. There is uncertainty in the markets, and insurance companies won't insure you because of pre-existing minor health conditions with one or two family members."

"You're right about that," I respond. "It's tough on a lot of families. Maybe what will eventually happen is that businesses, that are providing insurance to their employees, will come together and solve this problem."

Flat green fields mixed with low green humps have been whipping by. What we did not see in the dark while hunting for UFOs, east of Pierre, a couple of nights ago, we are seeing in the light of a bright day. The sky is unobstructed to the horizon. The terrain is similar to that leading to the Badlands and the Black Hills.

The hills and spires are way behind us now and we are moving ahead to skim Sioux Falls and turn north onto I-29. Nathan immerses himself in more Beethoven symphonies, coming through his headphones. At the same time he reads The Economist, the one magazine he subscribes to. It will be a couple of hours before we cross into North Dakota, and then another four and a half hours to Winnipeg, Canada. Dusk will be on us when we go through Canadian Customs.

"Kenny," I ask, "What are your favorite musical pieces and music groups?"

"Some of them are 'Fix You' by Coldplay, 'Boston' by Augustana, 'Look After You' by The Fray, 'Forever Young' by Alphaville, 'Burn' by Usher, 'Children of the Night' by Happy Hardcore, 'Slow Jamz' by Twista, 'Wonderful' by Everclear and 'Some Day My Prince Will Come' – song from Snow White."

"I haven't heard of any of them, except the song from Snow

White, which I like also. What kind of groups are they?"

"Techno, R&B and names I don't know what to call them. Classical music is the only kind of music that I ever hear that I don't like."

"And classical music is what Nathan and I love."

"In case you wonder," Kenny says. "I don't care that I'm not listening to my favorite groups now."

I exit at Watertown, population 20,265 by the sign, where a water tower rises above bungalows and the flatness of earth. We are hunting for one of Nathan's father's childhood homes. His dad had asked him to look it up and he wants to respect his father's wishes. Nathan's father's father was in the Marine Corps and had a small house for his family here, as he recruited young men of the Dakotas for the military. Then he himself went to fight in Vietnam. We found the streets, but a trailer park has taken over. I can see Nathan is disappointed. He wanted to show honor to his family and ancestors, as the Japanese do, a culture that Nathan feels an uncanny part of. Change is sometimes hard to take. One hour later we are at the state border.

# CHAPTER 13

# NORTH DAKOTA

WELCOME TO THE VALLEY REGION is written in white under the yellow lettered NORTH DAKOTA in a curve. All on a backdrop of green with light green rays of the sun. The boys stand at their signposts for the photo, their shadows the length of their bodies and angling to the east.

This Valley Region part of North Dakota is the Red River Valley, a hollow in the earth that was once a glacial lake about 12,000 years ago. The lake left behind flat land, with some of the richest black soil on earth and the Red River of the North flowing through it. The Red River of the South, in Texas, flows through John Wayne's movie, Red River.

"Just remember the Red River Valley. And the cowboy that loved you so true," is ringing in my head.

"Hey guys," Nathan says. "The Red River of the North is rare in the States, in that it flows northward. It flows to a Canadian wetland, which eventually becomes a tributary to the Hudson Bay, where the polar bears and the beluga whales swim, dive and play. The Red River will accompany us all the way to Winnipeg."

"Whales have a wide range of vocalizations," I add. "Of all the whales, only the beluga whale's sounds can be heard above water. They are playful like we are. And they are highly sociable, Kenny, like you and Nathan are trying and learning to be. They move from pod to pod. Pod membership is rarely permanent which seems to be what is happening to you in college, Nathan."

"I have a lot of friends," Nathan responds, "but they are not solid friends. Even though I'm one of the best known kids on campus, for my brain and for my niceness."

"I have just a few friends," Kenny offers, "but I don't see them much. You're my best friend, Nathan. Sorry, Ethel."

"Maybe friends will come in time, Kenny," I say. "I've been working on that my whole life. They come and go. I have a lot of friends, but I feel like I'm often the one who makes more of an effort to be friends. And I long for them to be more solid."

Looking out to the sun mid-way down in the western sky, I ask, "Do you know which President hung out a lot in North Dakota?"

"President Theodore Roosevelt," Nathan answers. "Our 26th President. He was a little older than us when he first came to explore. He was an adventurer who loved it so much that he bought at least one ranch way west."

We go past Fargo and think of the movie by that name, with an actress I love, Frances McDonald. The barren terrain looks familiar. "I think the accents spoken in Fargo, the movie, are extreme and stereotypical," I suggest to the boys. "I have relatives from this state, who do not speak like that. But movies, and the theater for that matter, love to deal with stereotypes. It was a good movie, but too violent for my tastes."

"Violence is part of what most moviemakers use in films," Nathan resignedly says. "It's hard to avoid it. When I see it, I just dismiss it in my own head, if I choose to.  Most of the time I don't care."

"And you don't think it affects your neural network in bad ways?"

"Maybe, but that's impossible to measure," Nathan says. "I don't think so."

I look at Kenny who offers, "I think it probably does affect the brain and maybe our behavior, although I don't think it affects me. I'm not a violent person. I live by what I know to be moral. But sometimes I feel like my mind gets messed up. I hate being in that state of mind. I don't where to go with those feelings."

"Let's go to Bismarck," I tease. "Just kidding. We just don't have time to go six hours out of our way to see the capitol. Sorry, Kenny for interrupting. I do take what you said seriously and we can talk about it if you like. And sorry, Nathan, to you too. I know you really wanted to see Bismarck and probably did not appreciate my joke."

Directly west of Fargo, almost 200 miles, is Bismarck, the capital city of North Dakota. Dakota residents call their capitol building, the hub of state government, a skyscraper. It's 242 feet high and looks appropriately like a grain elevator where wheat is stored. Hundreds of those tall rectangular boxes are scattered across the state, as it leads the nation in the production of wheat and other grains. Coal deposits, gas and crude oil production also rank near the top in the nation. As does wind. North Dakota has the greatest wind resource of any of the lower 48 states. Electrical power generated by wind is, of course, now in big demand as a renewable resource. North Dakota exports 60% of it to the rest of the nation. The flat and open land makes for an ideal and non-protested use of the up to 56 mph wind. When the wind blows harder than that, the turbines shut down for safety. This state of only 634,677 people, the 48th least populated state in the U.S., is the biggest provider of food and fuel for the entire nation. It is the breadbasket to keep us fed and the stove to keep us warm. North Dakota's wealth is indeed in its rich black soil and its ever-present wind.

"Yay for the wind turbines!" I say, as we see a wind farm in the distance. "Forget the protestors of windmills in other parts of the country. Look at that design, guys. The three long narrow blades on the high posts, to me, look sleek and elegant, like a work of art."

"Capital Bismarck," Nathan calls out with authority, "was named for the first chancellor of the German Empire, by the Germans residing here. The continental rivals, Germans and French, both helped settle North Dakota."

Nathan continues, "Another towering structure is coming up that I do want to see. It has the distinction of being the world's tallest man made structure on land. It's halfway between Fargo and Grand Forks. When I was young, I read a book that ranked the tallest, biggest, largest, longest buildings, structures, rivers – you name it, in the world. Though some of those have changed through the years. I want to see the ones that I can."

"Sounds good, Nathan," I assent. "Let's do it. Okay, Kenny?"

"I'm okay with doing anything that you guys want to do."

A good half hour north of Fargo, I pull off of I-29 onto a gravel road, without a soul or car around. We turn onto another gravel road in the flatness and see the spire thrusting into the sky. We ignore the posted 'No Trespassing' sign, renegades that we all are.

A small building with a sign saying 'KVLY-TV11' and 'TRANSMITTER,' is sitting at the base of the tower. Four main pipes of red metal, positioned several feet apart in a square, extend straight up from the ground to 3,038 feet elevation. Supporting cross pieces attach horizontally and diagonally to all the posts. Several smaller pipes also extend up inside this open structure. The boys and I lie on the ground near the guy-wire anchors and look straight up. It is almost dizzying and I blink and look away to recover. Nathan attempts to get a good photo but he can't get the whole image in one shot. As the tower moves away from us, it appears to narrow at the top, so we can't see it from the base.

"Is this like the Doppler effect?" I ask Nathan, who won an award as the top physics student in his high school class. "Where there is a change in wave frequency and wave length of a sound, like a train whistle coming closer and then moving away? But in the context of light waves, instead?"

"No," he answers. "This has to do with simple optics."

With my amateur physics analogy shot down, the boys leap up and run off their pent-up energy down the road, past the 'No Trespassing' sign, and I pick them up in the van. In minutes we are back onto the highway that will take us past Grand Forks and onward to Canada.

Nathan told me later that there is a Doppler effect for light, but it involves the frequency of light, which in the visible spectrum corresponds to difference of color. It is used to measure the speed of stars and galaxies approaching or receding from us. But it doesn't apply to the visually narrowing TV tower, which we see as sitting solid against the stationary ground. The visual field on our retina receives an impression of a narrower and longer angle of the tower, as it recedes from us. The tower appears to be smaller the further away it gets.

We're bidding farewell to the optically receding Missouri River, where Lewis and Clark paddled their long canoes through North Dakota into Montana. And we're saying goodbye, for now, to the center of the free life for Huck and Tom - The Mississippi River. Its headwaters are southeast of us, just over the border in Minnesota. We continue to follow closely the flow of the Red River into Canada.

Kenny, alias Huck, has told us more than once on this trip that he doesn't want to go to school. Huck never went to school. Kenny says that he can earn money by playing poker.

Nathan, alias Tom, says that Kenny is like Jack Dawson on

the Titanic. He got on the boat by winning a poker game. And Jack said that you don't know what hand you're gonna get dealt next, so you take life as it comes to you. No worries. Just live in the moment. Find your own path and forget school.

The core of Nathan's being is his love of learning. From the time he can consciously remember, around age one, he has wanted to learn. Absorbing knowledge was his favorite pastime, whether it involved geography, history, prehistory, anatomy, chemistry, astronomy, botany or zoology. From memorizing the Periodic Table of Elements to drawing progressively more detailed freehand maps of the world, from researching the lives of all American presidents to understanding the connections between things, learning has continued to be his biggest passion. He drives himself to be industrious and to achieve. It is as if his brain is on overdrive, with all neuronal connections on fire with purpose and intention. His ideas and plans fill up the spaces. He is a leader like Tom.

The contrast between these boys is exceptional, and yet they are such good friends, as Tom and Huck were. Nathan wishes for more intellectually challenging camaraderie from Kenny than he gets. But Kenny, like Huck, is a loyal friend. Alone, and then as friends, they have each weathered society's demands to fit in. At times it has been a tough row to hoe. But they are developing into their own unique selves and are having good times along the way. Like today on our way to Canada.

And then Kenny's cell phone rings. We have hardly used our

cell phones, except early on, when Nathan was apprising a couple of their mutual friends in North Carolina of our whereabouts. The ringing jolts us away from our thoughts, and Kenny's conversation ends up being a further jolt.

We can tell by the way that Kenny talks that it is his parents. Both are on the phone, and when Kenny says goodbye we have an uncomfortable feeling.

"My parents want me home early," Kenny tells us. "They said that maybe you can get me to an airport or a bus. I'm flunking out of school and they're afraid I might not be able to go back to my university. They found a college in New England that is alternative and might take me. And they want me to visit the school."

Both Nathan and I grimace in disbelief.

"First off, I'm sorry you're flunking out when you thought you had passed your exams. But, Kenny that changes the trip," I say anxiously. "I don't know how we can do that. It sure does affect things. I don't want for us to feel further pressured to get you somewhere and then end the trip early. It would consume a lot of time and effort and miles and phone calls and Lord knows what to figure out the airport thing. Let's think about it and see how we feel tomorrow."

Nathan agrees out loud with me and I can almost read his mind that he's resolving, here and now, to ignore the request. I find out later that that was correct. In fact, he would have dismissed the request totally and gone on with our trip. But tension set in that we couldn't shake. The fun dissipated, at least for now.

# CHAPTER 14

# MANITOBA, CANADA

It's dusk when we pull into Emerson, Manitoba, and join the car queue for Canadian Customs and Immigration. Canada's red maple leaf flag and provincial flags and banners stretch in front of us. The Red River, to our right, has been a steady companion all through North Dakota. It now crosses the border without stopping at immigration. But we must stop.

The customs agent, dressed in a dark gray-green uniform with a cap to match, leans into my window and looks around. He asks the expected questions. "Where are you from? Where are you going? How long will you be in Canada? What is the purpose of your trip? Do you have any drugs? Are you carrying any guns? Do you have any plants or produce? May I see your identification, please?"

Nathan and I have our passports ready to hand him. Kenny hands over his North Carolina driver's license. Nathan had told him before the trip that it was best if he brought his passport, though it wasn't an absolute requirement, but he evidently forgot.

The agent looks over the documents and says that they want to question Kenny further. I pull off to the side as they instructed. I wait while Nathan goes with Kenny into the nearby building. I'm glad Nathan is with him. But now we have tension added to tension. Customs inspectors do have the power to ruin a trip.

About twenty minutes later, the boys come out and get into the van. They seem relieved.

"A lot of people were in the room," Kenny starts to tell me. "Nathan sat on a chair next to me and one guy talked to me. He was polite and direct. He looked me up on a computer that was faced away from me. I could tell they found me and were probably looking for a criminal record, which I don't have. They didn't find anything."

"Were you nervous?" I ask.

"I wasn't really nervous, except a touch nervous that they wouldn't let me into Canada. They told me I should bring my passport next time."

"I'm glad we made it through."

"We are too," they sigh with relief.

"Welcome to Manitoba!" I say, in celebration of our crossing.

I get back on the road and we see a sign in the near dark, cut to the shape of this province with the words, Bienvenue Au MANITOBA/ Manitoba Welcomes You, on a deep teal background. Nathan takes a camera shot of the tall rectangle with a notched triangle hanging off the upper right side. Kenny's upper body is a black silhouette of head and arm against the bottom left of the sign.

Manitoba was the first province created from the Northwest Territories in 1870, by declaration of their Federal government. Just like the Dakotas were carved out of the Louisiana Territory by our Federal government in the late 1800s. All of our states govern themselves, but they function and cooperate as part of the larger unit, the United States. The ten provinces of Canada all have strong regional values and identities, and operate like mini-countries within the larger Canadian Confederation. Canada has also retained three territories, whereas all of the U.S.'s continental territories were long ago made into states. The three territories, Yukon, Northwest and Nunavut, are in the northern part of Canada, with a geographic size almost equaling that of all the provinces. Together, they add up to a gigantic country. Only Russia and Antarctica have more surface area than Canada, with the United States in fourth place. North and east of all three Territories range hundreds of sizable islands in the Arctic Circle. They make it onto the map in Beaufort Sea, Hudson Bay and Baffin Bay reaching to the North Pole. Which brings us to Nathan. At age seven, he knew the names, spellings and locations of a dozen of these Canadian islands, and was able to draw them from memory.

Manitoba, from Manitou or spirit, is a mix of prairie grasslands like the Dakotas, boreal forest wilderness and tundra in the far north and pristine lakes scattered throughout the province. 10,000 years ago the aboriginal people (the Indians, Metis and Inuits) were the first to settle here and remain today. In the late 1700s, the Europeans arrived. Fur trading led to growing grain crops and raising cattle, then to making tractors and buses. The Canadians make movies here for the world's viewing, and they export comedians from all over Canada – Jim Carrey, Martin Short, Mike Myers, Marie Dressler, Mort Sahl and many more.

An hour after Customs, we are in Winnipeg, population 710,000 and provincial capital of Manitoba. A familiar and comforting Holiday Inn sign catches our eye and we check in. The hotel clerk asks Kenny if he's part of the family, after I say that Nathan is my grandson.

"Yes, he's part of our family," Nathan and I both assent. "Right, Kenny?"

"Yes I am," he says, with his sweet smile.

"It's so nice to be here in Canada," Nathan tells the clerk.

Months ago, when planning this trip, Nathan said he wanted to see Canada and say "Hi" to our northern neighbors. "Remember to show your hospitality to the Canadians," Nathan reminds us, as we head to our room. "I want us to be good representatives of our country. They disapprove of the war in Iraq, and they haven't shown America much love lately."

I settle in bed with my laptop, while the boys cross the street to eat at Dairy Queen. Nathan and Kenny told me, when they returned to our room, that I wouldn't have found anything there to eat. Though potatoes are a big crop in Manitoba, they didn't show up at the Queen's table in either mashed or baked. The boys each got an unintelligent chicken tender basket with fries. Nathan drew a map of Canada on his napkin, including all provinces and territories, and North Carolina and all the united states in between, for the cashier. The cashier and all the kitchen help were very appreciative and impressed.

The boys decided to say goodnight to me and to hang out downstairs. They wanted to talk, just the two of them, and feel the freedom of no Bush Administration and its repressive laws in the States. Well, that's why the draft dodgers came here in the Sixties, I am thinking. For Nathan and Kenny, I feel it's more symbolic than an actual personal repression that is released. But Nathan, for all his tenseness since the 'come home sooner' death knell to the trip this afternoon for Kenny – and for us by default - is relieved here in Canada. He sees Canada as having fewer rules and along with that, he feels a sense of peace.

Each of these boys, in their 'alone' world in the early years especially, had a tough time learning the social and institutional rules. They are still trying to figure them out. What are the rules? When and how and where do they apply? What happens if I don't know them and I don't follow them? It all makes for unwanted tension. They want a release from too many laws and rules.

The next morning, as the boys still lounge in bed, they tell me more about their evening, which seemed pretty harmless, considering the tense events of that afternoon. They hung out in the 'fancy lobby,' as Kenny called it, and talked about the trip and Kenny's having to go home and about girls. Nathan hadn't had time alone with his good friend since the Mississippi River in Iowa. He wanted release, not just from laws and rules, but from burdening schedules too. He felt annoyed with my insistence on rushing. He felt that I cared more for adjusting the schedule to Kenny's parents' wishes, than Kenny himself did. Nathan would have stayed in Manitoba another full day. And he would have ignored Kenny's parents' request. They came to bed around 11pm.

It wasn't until about a year later that Nathan told me that they also went to the hotel bar that night. Under Canada and Manitoba's laxer drinking age laws, the 19-year-old boys were of legal drinking age for the first time ever. So they couldn't resist ordering a beer, and chatting about Canada with the bartender. Kenny would have been fine with telling me at the time (he thought that I wouldn't mind), but it was Nathan's idea to not say anything. He saw it as a bonding time with Kenny and he wanted to keep it between them.

I pay the hotel bill of 95.76 Canadian dollars, which is 75.42 U.S. dollars. Even though North Dakota, where we just came from, and Manitoba are sitting on huge crude oil reserves (drilling down to the Mississippian geologic formations), our gas fill-up costs more here than in the States. The boys might be feeling less repressive laws here, but Canada has higher gas taxes. With money on the mind, Nathan takes the wheel for us to find the Royal Canadian Mint.

We're passing up everything else that Winnipeg has to offer because of the rushing. The Manitoba Legislative Building for one, with its Grecian high pillars, fronting a three-winged beige brick edifice and topped with a copper crown. This is the center of governance for the province. The Premier of Manitoba leads a unicameral legislature in the official languages of English and French. Nathan wants to see it, but I am feeling the need, more than

I wish, to compromise with Kenny's parents somewhat, by getting back a day earlier than we planned. We've already decided to ignore the request to put him on a plane. According to Nathan, our sense of freedom to see what we wish died.

Though freedom may have died, the stately elm tree survived. Hundreds of the graceful trees line the shady streets of Winnipeg, light filtering through a canopy of a variant of leaves – enormous and small, saw-tooth edged or wavy, rows double or triple. These variants are what saved them. While Dutch elm disease that is spread by the elm bark beetle has decimated elm trees in the U.S. for decades, the elm tree has survived in the cold of Manitoba. Some variants here seem to have an inherent resistance to the disease. Their resilient genetic material may help save the species. "Winnipeg," I call silently to the distant boulevard of trees, "your century-old urban elm forest is in our thoughts, if not our sights. May your traits of longevity and beauty pass on for centuries to come."

Nathan planned months ago that we would see the Royal Canadian Mint. This is the big attraction for him in Canada, besides just stepping foot in the country. One of Nathan's many serious occupations has been collecting coins and bills. By the age of three, when he already had a passion for the Presidents, he became intrigued with all the presidents on our money. When he was 12, he started his currency collection. The two main reasons for his interest in collecting money were history and art. The historical interest is the pictured presidents, scenes and noteworthy people, and also the historic interest of the money itself. What he looks for in art are the pretty designs and scenes and the interesting colors. He's especially fond of Brazilian pastels, the designs of Canadian animals and landscape, and Japanese historical figures. His oldest complete series of American paper money, a bigger paper size known as horse blanket notes, is from WWI in 1914. In 1928, the U.S. changed sizes from horse blanket notes to today's size. Nathan has collected both sizes of Gold Certificates, Federal Reserve Notes, U.S. Notes, Silver Certificates and Federal Reserve Bank Notes. His first coin of interest, when he was three years old, was the Eisenhower silver dollar. In middle school, his favorite coin was the Benjamin Franklin half-dollar, so he purchased every single mint and year of that coin, from 1948-1963. He has a complete collection of silver Roosevelt dimes by year and mint. He collects coins by the first year they were made. He has steel pennies made at the height of WWII in 1943, when copper was needed for the war, and he has silver nickels from 1942 to 1944, when nickel was also being used for the war. Value is determined by need and demand in the choice of metals and by the war demands! And the value of Nathan's collection is, in his words, 'a lot.'

Now, at age 19, he rarely collects. If he does, it is mostly new designs of coins and bills that interest him. He has removed himself, physically and psychologically, from his collection and keeps it in a safe place. He doesn't want to risk oxidation with exposure to people and hands and to pollution or to the risk of accidental loss.

"Whose face is on the $100 bill?" Kenny asks. "And what presidents are below that?"

"Benjamin Franklin." Nathan answers. Then in order of $50, $20, $10, $5, $2 and $1 he names off, "Hiram Ulysses Simpson Grant, Andrew Jackson, Alexander Hamilton, Abraham Lincoln, Thomas Jefferson and George Washington. Benjamin Franklin, of course, was not a president and neither was Alexander Hamilton. He was the first secretary of the treasury."

"And remind me of the mints you've been to," I say. "I know we've been to two together, in Georgia and North Carolina."

"The Dahlonega Mint in Georgia and the Charlotte Mint Museum on the hill in North Carolina. They both minted only gold coins in the mid 1800s because of the local gold deposits. The first gold rush in the United States was in the mountains of North Carolina. I've been to the Philadelphia Mint, which has moved twice and to the San Francisco Mint, which was temporarily closed. I have not seen the Denver, New Orleans, West Point or Carson City Mints. But, soon we will see the Royal Canadian Mint," he says with a smile.

Nathan passes the sprawling campus of the University of Manitoba to the east as we pick up Bishop Grandin Boulevard. We cross our recent and welcome friend, the winding Red River, to get to Lagimondier Boulevard (I love the French names and spellings), and there on a rise is the one and only Mint in Canada.

They press all the coins used in Canada, one billion per year, as well as the coins for sixty countries around the world. It has a 'mint condition' reputation for its innovative technology and the impressive detailed design of its coins. It's respected worldwide as the standard in minting today.

We walk onto a plaza with a fountain splaying water up, and then dropping down to a circulating pool, like a weeping willow arches its branches. At the entrance, a canopy of transparent, connecting rectangles, framed in wood, is overhead. Inside the glass structure, designed by the local but world-famous architect Etienne Gaboury, is a high atrium where we are greeted with an octagonal, blue pool, or pond as the local greeter calls it. A concrete rectangle, holding green leafy plants is embedded in the center of the water. An array of luxurious plants fills the rest of the atrium space.

Beyond the atrium, are displays of collector coinage for sale, and further on is a gold bar, chained to the table, with its own guard standing at attention. Nathan is exuding happiness. He's in his element. The kind gray-haired, uniformed man in a light blue shirt and black pants is loaded down with insignias, walkie-talkies, long cords, nametag and dangling keys. He smiles with an offer.

"Would you like to lift the gold bar?" he asks Nathan, who is looking at it with interest. "It weighs 28 pounds and is made of solid 24-Karat gold."

Nathan represents we Americans well, with his gratefulness, sweetness and eagerness. He holds the foot-long, gold bar and poses and smiles, with the guard for my camera's eye.

"How much is it worth?" we ask.

"About 250,000 Canadian dollars," he answers.

"Mmmm," we all respond. We imagine in our own ways, what that would be worth in American dollars (around $200,000), to each of us.

On the other side of the blue pool is a long stretch of large windows looking onto the manufacturing facility. We peer through the glass and everything looks so clean, efficient and modern. Canadian coins are made of nickel-plated steel and copper-plated steel. Foreign coins are made of whatever metals a country requests. Collector coins are made of silver, platinum and gold. The production of all their coins takes place on this same floor level. It includes dye production, blanking, rimming, and checking for errors and more. The Mint's innovative plating process and multi-ply technology, that allows electromagnetic signatures to be embedded in the coins, is not for public view.

Gold - chemical element Au, atomic number 79, atomic weight 196.9665, deep yellow, soft, very dense and called aurum in Latin for glowing dawn - is still the public's most precious metal on the periodic table and has symbolized wealth and guaranteed power since the first civilizations began. Archeologists discovered gold jewelry in Egyptian tombs dating back to 3,000 B.C. Gold was found in artwork in the Persian Empire and gold artisans flourished in ancient Rome. Goldsmiths from pre-Columbian cultures in the Americas were master craftsmen, and gold was discovered in

California, triggering the Gold Rush of 1849. Thousands of settlers risked their lives to find gold, as we have been reminded on this trip. Gold has been the symbol of kings and pharaohs and the treasure of nations. Aristotle, in 500 B.C., pondered and concluded that gold is the perfect medium for money.

The gold standard, requiring countries to back up their currency with gold, stood us in good stead from the 1800s on, but all the countries participating in the world economy, including the U.S., abandoned the gold standard by 1971, when President Nixon ended the trading of gold with other countries. Most countries could not afford a gold standard and we could not afford to sell them gold from our dwindling reserves. Today, all countries keep reserves of major currencies instead of gold. The United States is part of a global economy, after all, that we want to keep stable and we have to maintain some standard. But gold, the romance of the past and of the present is of dependable value in reserves held by central banks and in private stores of wealth.

We finished our viewing and there is nowhere else to go. Whatever is above the ceiling in the tall pyramid of triangles that we are in, we are left to wonder. If it's a secret stash of wealth, we don't see it from the outside of the building, either, looking up and in. Green trees and a blue, sun-lit sky are mirrored on the reflective surface of the huge triangles of glass. Nature's wealth is with us now.

"What did you think of the mint?" I ask Kenny, as we get back into the van.

"I didn't think it was interesting. I liked how the pool looked. It's pretty big for an indoor decorative pool. The manufacturing was a bit interesting and I liked the water."

We know from what Kenny has said several times, that he is here on this trip because he wants to be here with us. He's interested in our company, but not so interested in the things we are seeing.

Fermor Avenue, which is also 35, which is also Highway 1, which is also the Trans-Canada Highway, is at the foot of the Mint's rise. Nathan follows the black number '1' on a white maple leaf that is directing us east. We'll keep going this way for hours to come, across Manitoba and the entire lower width of Ontario, to Lake Superior.

Accelerating our schedule from the original plan doesn't suit a mind like Nathan's, so he's tense and irritable. Nathan has intentions and plans, like wanting to see Lake Winnipeg, a long, narrow freshwater lake north of the city and where the Red River empties its flow. He wants to do what he expected to be doing, and that includes having the freedom to make this trip longer. He's usually able to ride the waves of change when he thinks it's absolutely necessary. But changing our plan for Kenny does not suit him, or me for that matter. I am caught in the middle and am rushing the trip by a day.

I thought of Tom Beck back in Indiana, rushing our van rush job when we rushed in and before he rushed work on the other rush jobs. It's really kind of funny if you can have a long perspective on the foibles of life and just laugh. But it's hard to laugh at a broken highway.

This grand sounding Trans-Canada Highway is four-lane and in decent shape for now. But we know it will shortly become two-lane for the rest of Manitoba, and all across Ontario, and the macadam will deteriorate along with the narrowing of the highway. The speed limit soon becomes 90 kph or 55 mph, just when we need to go faster. I hope the deterioration in the road doesn't symbolize the emotional state in this van, at least for long. I'll try to keep our spirits up.

"Remember the good old days in South Dakota?" I cheerily ask. "Four-lane, mint-condition highways to ourselves at 75 mph, with nothing to slow us down."

"I don't care," Nathan responds. "If I have to wait for a line of trucks, it doesn't matter. I don't care if we are slowed up."

Kenny is of the nature to go along with anything, as long as it doesn't interfere with his sense of freedom. So he is, on the surface anyway, happy and pleasant as always.

Speaking of freedom, even Nathan, who loves Kenny as a friend, says that Kenny takes his own freedom and liberty to an extreme degree and doesn't do what most people do, which is to self-improve and expand the limits on their lives.

Well, right now, we have our own practical limits to deal with, besides the speed limit. We won't be seeing the pristine Ontario lakes up close, or the quaint towns along the way, or have time to enjoy the 'beautiful nature,' as Nathan says, along Lake Superior. Although we have a tent and sleeping bags, we won't have time to camp along the shores of Lake Superior. But, that has been true this whole trip. There are always a zillion more things that we would want to do and see if we didn't have time constraints. We figured on this trip taking us about ten days, maybe more, and if it's going to end a little earlier than we wanted, let's deal with it.

There is frankly, not much to see on this stretch of eastern Manitoba, except barren land. The lakes and forests start in Ontario. The few deciduous trees, that we see, have barely begun to leaf. And the prairie fields are gray, reflecting the gray mood in the van. But with a little rise to the land, we start to see more lakes and forests, as we near Ontario.

# CHAPTER 15

# ONTARIO, CANADA

On to Ontario! Ontario, where the number on the maple leaf road sign changes from '1' to '17,' but the road remains the Trans-Canada Highway.

As Nathan says with a slight smile, we are so concerned with maintaining our speed that we passed up the sign welcoming us to Ontario. It was a rectangle flash of white and blue, like the sky, saying Welcome to ONTARIO More to discover. And Kenny wonders what the more is to discover.

Are things looking up? We hope so! The rising land, the blue flash of a sign against a sunny blue sky and a little humor sprinkled around, all lift our spirits. With the welcome sign promising us new discoveries, we roll along and what do we see to the side of the road, but a beautiful blue lake shimmering in the sunlight! We drink in the serenity. A few miles down the road is another lake with a backdrop of dark evergreen.

Ontario, from the Great Lakes in the south to Hudson Bay in the north, is BIG. You could fit in Montana and Wyoming easily, with a Dakota to spare. And it is filled with water and trees. Four of the five Great Lakes straddle the American border with Ontario, and all five (including Lake Michigan), make up the world's biggest continuous body of fresh water. Besides all that water on its borders,

Ontario has 250,000 pristine, fresh-water lakes spread throughout the province. These lakes are the result of Pleistocene glaciation more than 10,000 years ago. The retreating masses of ice carved their way through the bedrock of the Canadian Shield, leaving massive cliff faces above the waves. The Canadian Shield cuts a wide swath across the center of the province and takes up two-thirds of Ontario. This Precambrian rock dates back three billion years, the oldest rock in the world, and is rich in minerals. Three-quarters of the land is covered by Boreal forest of jack pine, spruce, poplars, birch and white cedar. Much of Ontario is unpopulated, so it is a pure, uncorrupted wilderness. The climate is harsh and the environment is hostile to human habitation, the further north you go, making it inaccessible to the modern world. Nature is free to be.

Right on cue, providing evidence of this being nature's home, Nathan calls out, "See the bear!" A black adolescent bear is looking at us, like any human would do, before it crosses the road. It lumbers across on hefty legs, and then starts climbing the embankment on the other side as we pass. We are thrilled to see a black bear on the loose.

"We can wonder if it's a she-bear or a he-bear," Nathan contemplates, "but let's just bear with our ignorance."

"It's a fact," I say. "Black bears live all over Ontario." In fact, they number 100,000 strong, and the numbers are growing.

There are no grizzly bears in the province for the black bears to compete with for food. Bears spend most of their time foraging for food and that's what this teenager bear is probably doing. They usually avoid humans, but we are glad to be in the safety of the van anyway. From what we have read and from the stories we have heard, if we did encounter a bear in the wild, we would slowly and quietly back away while watching the bear, to make sure it isn't following us. If it sees us, we would speak in a firm voice, and raise our arms to show we are a human and look as big as possible. The same goes for running into a mountain lion.

My cousin, Neal, in the Northern California wilderness, was carrying a bow saw and a branch in his right hand and a jug of water in his left hand, while walking back to his houseboat. When he looked to his left, he saw a mountain lion, sitting calmly and non-threatening, looking at him from about fifteen feet away. Neal was startled but didn't want to stop that close to a lion! He said very casually and matter of fact, "Oh, you're a wild kitty, aren't you." He continued to keep looking at the lion while walking backwards to his boathouse. We are not supposed to run away from predators, my cousin would say or they will chase us, thinking we're wild game. And don't climb a tree, since mountain lions and black bears can climb faster. If they come closer, we should yell and wave our arms, and if necessary, fight back with everything we've got. When my cousin got close to his houseboat, he kept looking at the lion and waved his bow saw around in an aggressive manner, as one might shake a fist at a person. The lion got up and started to walk toward Neal, but not in a threatening way. That is, his ears were not laid back, his tail was not thrashing back and forth and he didn't crouch, which would have preceded a leap or a jump. The lion kept walking toward him and Neal hollered and shouted at him loudly and with hurricane force, "No!" The lion stopped cold and Neal commenced to walk backward - or back pedal, as he would say - the rest of the way to his houseboat. The lion didn't follow any further. Neal went into his houseboat, where, as Neal said, "I was safe – right?!" After about five minutes Neal went out and up his gangplank to see if the lion was still around. The lion had moved onto a log about 40 feet away, so he could see where Neal went into his houseboat. The lion was sprawled out horizontally on the log. Neal picked up a club and pounded on a bay tree trunk really hard like a rifle shot. He was trying to impress the cat that it was unwise to attack him. He did that several times, while they watched each other, and then the lion lost interest and left. His leaving was all that Neal wanted to see. But the lion was in Neal's head for days after.

I've imagined myself many times reacting in a similar way with a mountain lion or a bear, while hiking the trails of California's wilderness parks. I put myself through the mental drill of what to do, so that my reflexes would react properly in such a situation.

Three weeks after our trip, Nathan was backpacking with his friend Paul in Sleeping Bear Dunes in Northern Michigan. He saw tracks of a man and his dog, and following them in a zigzag fashion were mountain lion tracks. Nathan prepared himself, in case, with driftwood in one hand and his Swiss army knife open in the other.

The lion may have been just over the next sand dune, but Nathan didn't see it.

Though both Nathan and Kenny take risks that I wouldn't take, they both have survival smarts and skills way beyond mine. There is a kind of animal instinct and awareness inside both of their bodies and heads that I admire, and it could serve them well if their lives are ever on the line. Is it the fearlessness they seem to have been born with? Or maybe it is their feeling of being one with nature, and animals respond in kind. Their loner status in early years might have honed them to be in touch and familiar with their primitive side.

"It's not just the bears," I tell the guys. "Geology, too, is oozing out of Ontario's pores; including the frigid, Precambrian rocky swath north of us across the province. Do you feel like naming off the geologic time chart, Nathan, to remind us?"

"Eons are divided into Eras, which are divided into Periods, which are divided into Epochs. But some categories have changed from what I learned in elementary school. The Precambrian Period is an outdated term because we now have a lot more fossil evidence to delineate early prehistory with more specificity. But the Precambrian was before the Cambrian Period, which was before the Ordovician Period, which was before the Silurian Period, which was before the Devonian Period (the age of fishes), which was before the Mississippian Period, which was before the Pennsylvanian Period, both together called the Carboniferous Period (the age of amphibians), which was before the Permian Period (the age of reptiles), which was before the Triassic Period, which was before the Jurassic Period, which was before the Cretaceous Period, which was before the Tertiary Period (the age of birds and mammals), which was before the Quaternary Period (the age of us). The Cambrian Period started 540 million years ago, and anything before that is in the Precambrian Period. The age of rocks help tell us when the earth was formed. I know the three Eras after the Precambrian Period - the Paleozoic, the Mesozoic and the Cenezoic Eras. I also know all the Epochs in the Cenezoic Era."

Kenny is mildly interested. He also overheard this a few days ago when Nathan was teaching his eight- year-old brother, over the cell phone, about these categories.

"Thank you, to you and your encyclopedic brain," I tell Nathan.

"Those were my favorite books from kindergarten through last semester," Nathan says eagerly.

"My brain is full. I can't hold anymore for now," I say. "Your brother is a lucky kid, learning from you."

What fascinates Nathan about the geologic time chart is seeing the entirety of the earth's history, especially of its life forms. He learned the periodic table when he was in fifth grade because he wants to know the nature of things. He has a store in his memory bank of countless other tables and charts and timelines, because he likes to order events, categorize things and systematize facts. That intense interest has been contagious, so now his 17 year-old brother has been 'infected', a word Nathan uses. And my own life-long, abundant curiosity about the world has stretched even further, with Nathan's infectious appetite for knowledge.

We nudge further along this slow, truck-lined highway, and watch for a good place to take a break. And what is before us, but another beautiful lake shining in the sun! Nature is giving us yet another gift.

Next to the water is a small white building, a general store, which I ask Nathan to stop at for gas and food. We all remember to put on a good face for America, so we're friendly and nice to the clerks and patrons, as we amble through the small store looking for something to our liking. "We like the quiet in this part of the country." "The lakes and the trees are beautiful." "Yes, we're from the States." "We're enjoying our stay in Canada." "Thank you for your hospitality!"

I buy fruit, raisins and nuts, to squirrel away for the rest of the trip. Just as the black bears do, with their love of fruit in the summer and hazel nuts and beechnuts in the fall.

"Thank you very much." "Have a great day."

I didn't want to insult them with bad French so I did not dare to say, "Au revoir, a la prochaine fois." The boys, who would have spoken French well, chose to speak English, "Goodbye until next time." And we wave and swing out the door. Outside, the boys remind me that French is spoken mainly in Quebec. So I quietly rejoice that I didn't attempt my French on English-speaking Canadians.

Nathan has driven at least half way across Ontario on our route to Lake Superior. We all felt that it was better that Kenny not drive in Canada, without his passport. So I'll take us the rest of the way until I decide to call it a night. My turn at the wheel seems endless, but I'm motivated to get as far as we can. There isn't much we would have stopped or gone out of our way for on this stretch, even with time on our hands.

Nathan is happy that I'm taking over. He and Kenny can talk and I'll just listen or let my thoughts wander. But I'll keep my attention on the road. You need it on a two-lane road, with trucks barreling along and spewing exhaust by the way – are there no emission standards in Ontario? And I must watch for unexpected potholes in our path. Let the guys forget all that stress and just talk.

I think it's Kenny's acceptance of Nathan's wishes that makes this friendship work. Nathan is glad to do what he himself wants, and Kenny is happy to have someone leading the way. That works in conversation too. Nathan puts the ideas and streams of information out there, and Kenny can comment when he wants. And of course, there are the arcade and board games and physical exertions of hiking and climbing that they do together. But they really bond when they commiserate about their travails in the peopled world and how to navigate through it.

If I could tolerate navigating this highway for hours longer than our plan, and drove to the eastern edge of Ontario, we would reach Ottawa, the capital of Canada. Nathan had wanted to visit Ottawa, but it was not in the plan, thank goodness. Nathan would love visiting the Canadian capitols almost as much as the American capitols He considers the United States and Canada to be one country.

Ottawa is the capital of Canada as Washington D.C. is the capital of our United States. But to look at Parliament Hill, Canada's governing headquarters in Ottawa, you would think you were in London. Ottawa's Parliament building looks like a less weighty version of Parliament in London. Gothic towers spread out along a high gray rectangle of stone and windows, with a very tall clock tower in the center, and capped with a blue-green patina copper cone. The Sovereign, the Senate and the House of Commons reside there. The Sovereign Queen Elizabeth II and her Governor General, for all practical purposes, let the Prime Minister of Canada govern the country. Paul Edgar Philippe Martin is holding that office right now, as leader of the Liberal Party of Canada. A large English country cottage of a building sits separately on the Hill to house the Supreme Court of Canada. The Library of Parliament, also on the Hill, sits like an ornate crown designed in a High Victorian Gothic Revival style of architecture.

But we're not there and their way of governing is almost too complicated to think about right now.

I'm passing by some of those quaint towns that Nathan had hoped to see. English River, Upsala (Swedish like the town of

Uppsala, where my relatives are from), and Finmark where the Finns emigrated. Then it's an hour drive to Thunder Bay.

Nathan spotted Kakabeka Falls on the map a while ago, and now makes a case for a stop. "Let's go to Kakabeka Falls. It's the second highest waterfall in Ontario after Niagara Falls."

I was a little reluctant because of time, but he talked me into it with "We need a break and some exercise," and I'm glad he did.

I passed the town of the Finns and in 20 minutes we were at the falls. Kakabeka comes from the Ojibwe word gakaabikaa, meaning 'waterfall over a cliff.' The falls drop 40 meters (131 feet), and cascade into a gorge carved out of that Precambrian Shield that Ontario is famous for. Fossils 1.6 billion years old are in that rock.

The rushing sound overtakes you before you even see the water. We take a trail to a jutting platform, and there it is, looking almost as big as Niagara Falls. The Kaministiquia River is above us pouring water into the falls. Looking down, we see the white clouds of foam hitting the rocky chute below.

The trail takes us along the gorge and we get the full impact of the size and sound of the falls. It's a sunny day, about 60'F, and the walking and climbing stimulate our blood flow. We all have a pink flush, and Nathan and Kenny are having a grand time. I am taking in the beauty of nature and the boys' joie de vivre.

"Thanks, Nathan," I say, "for wanting to see the falls. I'm glad you persuaded me."

The three of us walk back to the van together, arm in arm.

Within 20 minutes we make it to Thunder Bay, Lake Superior and Highway 61 all at once. Thunder Bay is Canada's westernmost port on the Great Lakes. And it is one of Canada's busiest, with its large bay for logs and lumber, grain storage and shipbuilding.

Lake Superior is the largest freshwater lake by surface area in the world. We're going to follow the upper edge of its chicken wing shape, to the tip of the wing in Duluth, if I can make it that far in an alert state at the wheel.

Highway 61 begins in Thunder Bay and crosses into the U.S. at the Pigeon River Bridge. It then becomes Minnesota State Highway 61 all the way to Duluth. Bob Dylan sang about this road in Highway 61 Revisited - 'And they were both out on Highway 61.' Well, make that three of us out on 61. Pretty scenery takes us all the way back to the U.S.-Canada border.

"We're less than a half hour from customs, guys," I warn. "Have your identification ready."

"I want to tell you my philosophy on borders," Nathan starts up, "especially the one between the U.S. and Canada. Our governments should allow people and goods to cross borders freely. I want those border stations completely dismantled, all tariffs abolished, and all useless hassle like this to be eliminated. As far as security against terrorists goes, if the U.S. and Canada had a unified defense, as in coast guard, border guards and immigration patrol, training and working together, sharing personnel and information, then our mutual security would be far higher than with this silly exercise in blocking roads. Let's go down the list of 'prohibited' or 'restricted' items. Most of those are just for the governments to make a quick buck. Plants and animals: It may stop diseased beef, but nothing else important. Plus, we need to solve the problems inherent in factory farming. Firearms: Why can't I go hunting in Canada? I suppose our crime might spill over into Canada, but it has already spilled into places like Windsor and Vancouver. Drugs and alcohol: This isn't going to stop anything. Everyone with drugs lies, while alcohol is nothing but a grab at your wallet. I think that these border stations are an affront to the personal liberty at the heart of both countries' foundations. We should erect an American Schengen. That is the European open borders agreement."

After a pause, Nathan jokes, "You're an outlaw, Kenny. Where shall we hide you? The border patrol might take you away."

"How does it feel to be an outlaw?" I ask.

"Free," Kenny says. "Because I'm outside the law."

Less than a mile from customs, the boys spot the Ontario sign on the other side of the highway going north. We agree in a split second to go back and not miss this photo-op like we did many hours ago when entering this province. After pulling a fast U-turn, I sheepishly suggest, "I guess I'm the outlaw now, guys. This is a daring move just before we see all those border patrol agents."

I rest the van and we jump out onto the side of the highway in front of the kitchen table-sized rectangle on small wooden posts, shadows angling to the right. There would have been barely a shadow from the sign way back on the Manitoba border. With his left hand, Nathan takes a photo of his right hand, thumb up and fingers clenched into a 'good for us' gesture, in front of the Welcome To ONTARIO More to discover sign. The More to discover will have to wait for another trip, another time. I defy the Canadian law one more time with another U-E and go south to the border.

# CHAPTER 16

# MINNESOTA

We clear customs without a hitch, Kenny in full view. I guess the good old U.S.A. is glad to have us back. And I, for one, am glad we made it all the way from Winnipeg to the U.S. in one day.

Minnesota Welcomes You! Says the imposing gray granite sign. Nathan and Kenny leap from the van and climb up the five-foot tapered brown and gray fieldstone base. They stand tall in front of the gigantic granite shape of the state. The granite is several inches thick and sits solidly, without visible support, on a stone base. What strength this state shows. The low western sun lights the boys up and I snap the picture-perfect moment. Nathan is in his long black pants and orange-fading-to-gold knit shirt to match the setting sun, and Kenny wears his white shorts and light blue T-shirt to match the sky. Minnesota is written in bold, cranberry red script. It makes a splash of brightness amidst the subdued colors in my camera's frame, just as the state's cranberry bogs splash color across the flaxen landscape.

The wild rice paddies in northern Minnesota, that have helped to fill my rice cake needs, are being replaced by the cranberry bogs, as Minnesota attempts to compete with the Wisconsin and Massachusetts markets.

Minnesota is a new state to mark onto both Nathan and

Kenny's lists. I've been here dozens of times, since it borders Wisconsin, the state where I grew up. Minnesota is the land of 10,000 lakes within its borders, and Lake Superior makes a border of its own with Minnesota, Michigan, Wisconsin and of course Ontario.

Forests of pine, spruce and fir, where the gray wolf, lynx and woodland caribou make their home, cover the eastern side of the state abutting Lake Superior. The shoreline areas are stopover sites for migrating waterfowl, shorebirds and land birds. Moss and lichen cling to the steep cliff faces and rare Peregrine falcons breed and hunt from their cliff habitats. Lake Superior, along with the other Great Lakes, was a transportation route through which humans have passed for over 4,000 years.

My forebears from Sweden made their way by ship, from the Atlantic Ocean through the Saint Lawrence River, 125 years ago. The Lachine Canal, and other canals and locks, built in the 1800s, helped navigate ships and boats through the rapids and shallows, and then over these Great Lakes. My ancestors settled in the pine-rich land in west-central Wisconsin to join the lumbering crews and to start families. I tell this to the boys. It's part of my history and of Nathan's and a history that is shared with many European-descent Midwesterners.

The waterfalls and rivers, the rolling hills with dense evergreen and white birch, are all part of the beautiful nature that Nathan wished for. The cliffs, interspersed with a low rocky shore, form the basin for the lake. The basin is cut out of that Canadian Shield, three billion years old that extends from Ontario into northeastern Minnesota. We can see the shoreline, through the trees, sloping down toward the water. The lake is frozen a good ways out, and then the white ice changes to dark blue ice-cold moguls of water.

In spite of the cold and ice, we consider setting up our tent along the shore. It is the month of May, after all, and our sleeping bags are warm. But our better sense wins out with the setting sun. It's cold now and only going to get colder through the night.

As we drive on, it becomes pitch dark without any highway lights to brighten the path. But then, nature on cue reveals the beauty of the moon, rising and shining brightly on the ice, and sparkling on the waves. It is a half-moon, waxing on its way to a full corn planting moon or flower moon or milk moon, all in the month of May. Naming the moons is how the Algonquin Indians, part of the larger Anicinape grouping of Indians that spanned from New England to Lake Superior, kept track of the seasons. And the waxing moon is a time of beginnings.

But this is the ending, the waning, not waxing, for us, of a very long day. The moon's light is suddenly taken over by city lights. We have reached the tip of the wing of water, Duluth, Minnesota. Its sister city, Superior, Wisconsin, is just across the border, both important port cities on Lake Superior. On Superior Street, a familiar Super 8 sign greets us. Super-ior all the way, we are ready and longing for a good rest. I shower and sit in bed luxuriously with my laptop, then Kenny takes over the bathroom for his favored soak in the tub. On the other side of the wall lamps, Nathan sits in his bed and again reads from his favorite book The Emperor of Japan: Meiji and His World.

"The Meiji was only 15 years old when he ascended the Imperial throne, after his father, Emperor Kohmei, died in 1867," Nathan tells me. "He took Japan from a feudal nation to a modern state, on par with Europe and America. What I admire is that he was committed to world peace, prosperity and the well being of all, not just the people of Japan. He oversaw the military maneuvers and subjected himself to the same conditions as the common soldier. He donated money to people suffering from earthquakes, as far away as Taiwan and San Francisco."

"You look just like him," I comment, looking over at the Meiji's full-bodied picture on the book cover.

"I see my resemblance absolutely to him in all his pictures. I'm proud of that. I really like that. I use him as my profile picture on Facebook." The Meiji Emperor is probably the only person who Nathan holds in higher esteem than President Truman.

An hour later, we turn out the lights. Sleep comes easily for all of us.

On my awakening the boys, Nathan makes this observation from bed to us: "We, on this trip, have laid siege to all the states around Minnesota, and only now have we breached the Minnesota castle walls. Wisconsin, Iowa, South Dakota, North Dakota, the Canadian provinces of Manitoba and Ontario, all making a border, and now Minnesota itself."

"You're right!" I say in surprise. "And the castle wall metaphor fits in with the strength that Minnesota seems to exude. All this ancient rock, and big ships in the harbor and the strong pioneering spirit of the original Scandinavian settlers."

After a continental breakfast, we find I-35 for the 2-hour drive to the Twin Cities. Kenny is the driver now. It's been a long time, what with his 'outlaw' status, and he is eager to be at the wheel.

"You're in charge now, Kenny," I say. "Take us where you will."

Nathan, usually the navigator on this trip, is sitting in the back and says nothing. We know from the impatience he has shown recently, that he is tired of doing most of the map guiding. So Kenny stops, spends time with the map and figures out the route all the way to the State Capitol building in Saint Paul.

It's Tuesday, and we're under the gun to get Kenny home to North Carolina by Thursday night. He and his parents plan to visit a college in the Northeast on Friday. That certainly doesn't ease Nathan's impatience or my sense of urgency, but I'll try to forget all that and enjoy our few remaining days. Kenny metaphorically rides the waves, just as he's smoothly rolling us along on the highway.

I've done some reading of Edgar Cayce in the past few years, and he says that in whatever situation you find yourself, it is what is necessary for your development. So what does this situation call for? Patience? Negotiation skills? A calm spirit in the midst of troubled waters? I think my own development could use a little letting go. To let go is what I am going for.

Except that I do want to mention people who have not had much of an education. So I tell the boys, "Kenny, I understand your parents wanting you to go to college, and their concern with finding a place where you can succeed. Education is important for all of us, whether it comes from formal school or lifelong experience. I think the general thrust of our psyche and brain is to improve ourselves. I, for one, encourage formal education very strongly. You, Kenny, want to teach yourself and learn on your own.

"You don't like to be in a classroom with grades and tests," I continue, "but what learning are you doing on your own? You don't have to answer. Just think about it.

"Some people do make it on their own. President Lincoln, whom we plan to visit tomorrow, never went to formal school until he started studying law. Benjamin Franklin never went to school, but learned plenty on his own. Our good friend, Harry Truman, graduated from high school, but had no opportunities to go further, since he couldn't pay for law school. Albert Einstein despised formal schooling because it was unchallenging. Like Nathan, Einstein didn't talk until he was three, and his parents were concerned that he might be retarded."

"That just proves," Nathan said, "that you can be really smart, but not show it in the usual expected ways."

"My own dad needed to stop school in eighth grade," I added, "in order to help his family survive on the farm. But, he continued to read ravenously and improve himself until the day he died. A stack of philosophy and history books was in arm's reach from his favorite chair, at age 81.

"And Mark Twain, who we keep bringing up on this trip, had an aversion to school and stopped going when he was 12 years old. He created characters in his own likeness, Tom and Huck, who skipped school or never went to school."

"People do have to learn some on their own," Nathan asserts passionately. "The greatest paradox for me, is that I, who love learning more than anyone I know, absolutely hated most of elementary school and had disdain for middle school and high school."

"What do you think about that Kenny?" I ask.

"Education in schools is useless for me," Kenny responds. "Education can be very important, depending on your goals. As for myself, I'm not learning on my own, because it would be mentally painful to do so."

"How is it painful?" I ask.

"It's like running on a treadmill, past physical pain, and you keep going. But for me the pain is in my mind. It's too hard to think that hard. I hope to learn stuff in the future but I don't want there to be pain."

"Mmm," I sympathize. "I wish I could help you with that. But maybe you'll discover for yourself, as time goes by, what works for you. You certainly are bright and you know a lot. I hope you find something that you can be passionate enough about, that you'll want to learn more.

"Here's some learning for you, Kenny," I continue, looking out on the rolling pastureland. "Massive ice sheets covered Minnesota during the ice age 12,000 years ago. They missed only the southeast corner of the state where steep hills called bluffs channel the Mississippi. That is very near to where I lived in Wisconsin in what is called the coulee region of hills. Speaking of the Mississippi, its headwaters are just west of us now at Lake Ithaca."

"That kind of learning is fine but not necessarily useful," Kenny said.

"Bear with me, Kenny, here is some more learning," I added. "Minnesota is a very healthy state by many measures. The people are very healthy and they live longer here than in any other state except Hawaii. Education and the economy in this state rank high in the nation. Many publicly traded companies are headquartered here, including Target, where you worked briefly in North Carolina. And the political system is active and well."

"How do you know that?" Kenny asked.

"I learned some from books and some from talking to people," I answered.

Kenny pulls into downtown Saint Paul and we see the State Capitol.

"What's the population of Saint Paul, Kenny?" I ask.

"262,000," he answers.

"How did you know that?"

"Like I said before. I memorized the whole table of populations and other tables that were in an Almanac several years ago. It was by accident. I would look at the populations because I was interested, but I did not try to memorize them. I memorized them by consequence of looking at them a lot."

Kenny finds a parking spot on Cedar Street and we have a short walk to the capitol building. A stark white marble dome, resembling Michelangelo's Saint Peter's Basilica in Rome, sits on top of a light gray, long stone rectangle, with a gray chilly day as a backdrop.

Nathan needs a bathroom fast so he tears ahead. Kenny and I climb the broad granite steps and enter the halls of warm golden Kasota limestone, 450 million years old from southern Minnesota. The warm golden interior feels good after coming in from the chill gray outside. We hunt and wonder where Nathan is. There is not a sign of him as we wander the halls and climb the stairs. He seems to have made himself lost to Kenny and me and to our concern. At last we find him a couple of floors up and he is not eager to see us. He wouldn't talk at first, but then said he wanted to be by himself. He's still annoyed with both of us because of the rush. He did not like my getting them up earlier this morning than the agreed upon hour.

When Nathan was 12 years old, he was traveling with his family in Nevada and California. He wanted to see the Nevada Capitol building in Carson City, and while his family waited in the car, Nathan ran in and came out the other side and around to their car with amazing speed. The next day they did the same with the California Capitol building in Sacramento. But this time, Nathan did not come out. They were very worried for his safety and all went in to search for him. His father looked everywhere and at last found him in the dark, watching an informational film about California. Nathan was absorbed in his own world of learning, plus he had so much more to see in the capitol that interested him. He figured that his family would be able to wait or find something to do. He had no inkling that he had done anything to worry them. When Nathan first saw his father, he thought he was there because he was interested in the capitol too. But his father made him leave the movie, before it was over, to get back to their car. It was an upsetting experience for all of them. His mother decided then, that in the future she would start giving him a time limit.

Well, Nathan is 19 now, and acting very responsibly in so many areas of his life. But I did not expect him to deliberately lose us. I was both distressed and feeling a bit of sympathy for Nathan's reaction to the rush. There is no time or interest in tracking down Republican Governor Tim Pawlenty. Tracking down Nathan was enough.

Both boys do some impulsive things and have some unusual traits that might annoy people, but their actions are not beyond living with. And along with those unusual traits, are their unusual talents, which I admire immensely. But some people in society do not accept anything unusual in a kid, if it gets in the way of their normal living. They want cookie-cutter behavior and actions that fit in perfectly with what they expect. Critical looks and comments from adults, and rejection by peers, can be hurtful and devastating to an unusual kid trying to find his way. People can feel uncomfortable around a kid who twists his own neck. Or someone who does not meet their eye in conversation, paces the circle at circle time in preschool, speaks in a voice too loud for the situation or does not respond to commands or obey rules. These behaviors can elicit reaction ranging from awkwardness to intolerance.

Acceptance is the key. Both Kenny and Nathan crave it, and all people, I dare say, want universal acceptance of who they are. Please, whatever powers that be let us all be totally accepted by someone. It can be a hard world to operate in and we can all use some love for who we are.

Nature can help us immerse ourselves in sublimity. Maybe that's why both boys have such a love affair with the wild, and cherish animals and hiking and lakes. Here, wandering close by, as we return to the van, is our old friend from our first night in Iowa, the Mississippi River, where Huck spent most of his time in the novel Huckleberry Finn.

A riddle pops out of Nathan's mouth. "What did Mrs. Sippy drink? A mini-soda." His humor is back, thank goodness.

Our next stop is The Mall of America, the largest enclosed mall in the United States, but no longer in the world. That honor presently belongs to our neighbors to the north, in West Edmonton. The Bloomington, Minnesota structure covers seven acres and has an Amusement Park inside. Overhead is a gigantic supporting steel grid and a glass roof to let in natural light. It's noisy and busy with kids, but the rides look sappy according to the boys. They settle on the popular water-borne Paul Bunyan Log Chute. Nathan and Kenny survive shooting through a 70-foot mountain and taking two dramatic plunges 40 feet each, in a log. Next we see Paul Bunyan himself, standing 19 feet tall, with animated limbs and a deep voice. Paul is the fabled hero of the North Woods lumbering country. After saying goodbye to Paul, we leave the North Woods and hit the road, heading south.

"What's the population of Minneapolis?" I ask Kenny.

"355,000," he answers.

We cross the Mississippi and are back in Wisconsin. There are no more shots in my disposable camera, so we pass up the state sign.

# CHAPTER 17

# WISCONSIN

The familiar, rolling pastureland of Wisconsin is easy on the eyes, and the next three hours on the road are a wonderful respite from the pressure we've been feeling the last few days. From cool and gray, it's become a perfect May day, and we have done most of what we wanted to do.

"Nathan and Kenny, today is the 17th of May, and it is a very special day for me," I tell them.

"I know," Nathan says with a wistful tone in his voice.

"Carl and I were married forty-seven years ago, today, by the lilacs in the little white Baptist Church of my youth. Let's go to the lilacs at the Madison Arboretum, where eight years ago today, we tossed his ashes to the winds."

We are all silent for a long time, me with my memories. We pass near my childhood town, which brings up more memories. I give them silent homage. With a stop at one of Wisconsin's pristine waysides, Nathan takes over the wheel to drive the rest of the way to Madison. He circles around Capitol Square, so Kenny can see the Wisconsin State Capitol from the van. Nathan has already been there with his Grandpa Carl and me. It's the crown jewel for me, of all the capitols that we have seen. It is so full of beauty, and brings back memories of being a University student and of being a married woman to Carl with our three children.

Then Nathan heads for the Arboretum, and after passing prairie wild flowers, we reach the lilacs. It is a beautiful day and the flowers are in full and glorious bloom. White, pink, blue, deep purple and lavender lilacs show off their riches and engulf the air with their heady scent. In one open area surrounded by lilacs, is a crabapple tree in blossom, drooping its branches in homage over a freeform pink marble bench. Carl's name is engraved on a brass plaque on the side. Nathan wants to be by himself and he lies down on the bench. Kenny disappears into the fields of lilacs. He is a sensitive soul to others' feelings. I walk throughout the purple beauty far away from Nathan and breathe in the sweet intense fragrances. After a time that seems timeless, I'm aware that Nathan has left Carl's space, and I go over to spend a few minutes commiserating with Carl, myself. I see him clearly in my mind's eye and he says, "You're okay. I'm okay." The tears flow.

Nathan and I arrive at the van at the same time and Kenny again is thoughtful enough to stay in the fields. Nathan told me that Carl said several things to him. Nathan was lying on his back on the bench and he imagined his Grandpa's presence in the lilacs. Carl asked, "Do you want to get up?" Nathan sat up and asked, "Where do you want to go?" Carl answered, "Wherever you do." That's exactly what Nathan wanted to hear. After walking through the lilacs, Nathan lay down on his stomach on the ground. Carl then told Nathan, "When you were younger I told you not to cry. I'm sorry I said that." Nathan felt relieved and he cried, full of emotion, tears streaming down his face. Along with his tears, he was able to release much sadness from the past, including when his Grandpa Carl died. Then, Carl and Nathan got up from the ground next to the lilacs and walked on. That internal dialogue was important for Nathan because of restrictions he has felt all through his life, even ones that were totally arbitrary that he doesn't voice. In general, many restraints have been brought on him by other minds, as he sees it. People are sometimes unable to comprehend his feelings. With Carl, he was set free from the confinement.

"I still miss him," I said longingly. Nathan said that he did too.

The idea of having a bench somewhere, to remember Carl, formed in Nathan's 11-year-old-mind the day that his grandpa died. Now, with the bench as our communion place, we are remembering him in poignant ways. Through the tears and the flowers and the near-completion of our circuit, we feel healed.

Kenny is kindly quiet when he joins us in the car. We return to Nathan's college and the small college town where I am just starting to rent a house for one year. We make up the beds, eat supper and then do some catch-up on emails on the computer. Nathan checks online for his grades. He has kept up a near perfect 'A' average. Sleep is welcome. I've been riding a roller coaster of emotions today, and I have survived and become even stronger. My mind is at peace.

For the first time this entire trip, we sleep in. Well, for me, getting up at 8:30am is sleeping in. For the college guys, 9:15am is way too early. But everyone is so cheerful on arising it is a joy to behold.

"We have come such a long ways, guys. And we do have a ways to go, but we'll make it in good shape. Thanks for being so good about everything. The past ten days has been full of so many wonderful things."

"Yes," they agree.

"It was a good trip," Nathan says. "And I have more states and capitols to see."

"Let's celebrate with a restaurant sit-down meal. It's my treat," I offer.

Kenny has had a yen – or a yuan as Nathan would say in Mandarin - for Chinese food this whole trip, so I drive us to the Asia Buffet for an early lunch. They have a splendid array of egg drop and miso soups, egg rolls, garlic green beans, bean sprouts and other fresh Chinese market vegetables, as well as spicy chicken and beef. I pass by the warm aromatic desserts that a sugar lover, unlike me, would devour.

"Mark Twain might enjoy this," I say. "He was a vegetarian like me and there are so many choices."

"That was a hundred years ago," Nathan says. "This might be a little strange and exotic for him. If he ate 'out,' he probably ate edible roots and grasses on the banks of the Mississippi."

"I would eat that too," I say.

# CHAPTER 18

# ILLINOIS

Nathan drives three hours to Springfield, Illinois, home of President Lincoln and of the State capital. The young lawyer Lincoln was responsible for getting the fifth capitol building of six to be in Springfield. We'll see the sixth and perhaps final one. Nathan takes us south to Madison Street, past Jefferson, Washington, and Adams Streets, to Monroe Street. Nathan is right at home amidst these presidential avenues.

The capitol does not disappoint. After all of the gold and copper domes, we've seen, here we look up to an elegant silver dome. It sits on top of a six-sided tower, on top of a several story limestone base in the shape of a Latin or Christian cross. Depending on to whom you talk, the Capitol is designed in a French or Renaissance style. The dome thrusts higher than the U.S. Capitol in Washington D.C.

Inside, we go past murals and painted wall coverings, and under stained glass in the dome, to the third floor to find the Senate in session. Government is at work! Maybe even the Governor is here. Rod Blagojevich, as well as his neighbor to the north, Jim Doyle of Wisconsin, are both Democratic Governors of Midwestern states. The Senate has fifty-nine members, and at least some are multi-tasking at their roll-top desks, which conceal microphones, computers and push buttons for voting. We see the action on monitors and listen to the Senate leader summing up a case for some legislation. We walk in the halls and see a spillover of well-suited men and women buttonholing each other about urgent business, and lobbying for favors.

Our sense of urgency is just as urgent as those legislators in suits. We hurry to the van to drive past Lincoln's now restored fifth capitol building. Here is where he first confronted Stephen Douglas and where he delivered his famous 'A House Divided' speech. It is a modest brick building with four pillars and a small dome.

We are in, what Lincoln aficionados like my brother would call, sacred territory. Illinois is called The Land of Lincoln, after all. Our 16th President lived in Illinois, with his wife Mary Todd and their children, for nearly twenty-five years. He was born in 1809 in a log cabin in Kentucky, was President from 1861 to 1865 and was assassinated in 1865 at Ford's Theatre in Washington, when he was 56 years old. His legacy is a restored Union after the Civil War, with malice toward none. On January 1, 1863, he issued the Emancipation Proclamation that declared forever free, those slaves within the Confederacy, and all people within the reunited nation.

"Now that's freedom, you free-minded guys," I praise, as we talk about Lincoln's life and accomplishments. "And Lincoln started to bind the nation's wounds."

We stop and look at Abraham and Mary Lincoln's house on Jackson Street. It is a simple, two-story, white clapboard house, with green shutters framing all the windows, and sits so neatly on a flat square plot of land. A few trees are just beginning to leaf and blossom.

"There has to be a Lincoln bedroom in there," I say, looking up to the second story. "One that he really slept in and that is more modest than the one in the Washington D.C. White House."

"Abraham Lincoln and I are the same height," Nathan says, "6 feet 4 inches. His feet probably hung over the edge of his bed, like mine sometimes do. I can imagine myself living here."

"Maybe you could move in," Kenny said.

We make a stop at the National Park Service and Nathan has his special National Landmarks Passport stamped with the Lincoln site, amidst others stamps from travels past.

Nathan can't resist telling a humorous anecdote that he read in a book about myths in American history. "There was an exhibit that had a log cabin. The placard said something like this: 'Abe Lincoln was born in this log cabin, which he built with his own hands'."

"Next stop, Indianapolis," I say.

# CHAPTER 19

# INDIANA

We are taking a two-lane road, Highway 36, directly east, on our way to the very center of Indiana, the capital city of Indianapolis.

The boys are having arguments in the van, healthy debates, I hope. Nathan is arguing with passion, anger and frustration. Kenny is showing steady persistence with his point of view. One discussion is over costs of the trip. Nathan has been adding up all the costs from records, I have saved, and is doing the math. Tomorrow, our last day, he'll add on tomorrow's costs. Kenny thinks he should owe less than he does because we added on Wyoming and Montana. Nathan says we agreed before the trip to share equally the costs of gas and motels from Wisconsin on, however it adds up. Nathan points out to Kenny what he does not have to pay for, 6000 miles worth of wear and tear on the van. Kenny doesn't budge. I finally intervene.

"You should pay your share, Kenny," I say. "Which includes the whole trip together. We didn't know exactly how far we would go when we started. We all have to allow for a little flexibility in the itinerary, and pay accordingly."

"I am not going to pay the extra," he says with determination.

We let the discussion go for now, but later we do resolve it to everyone's satisfaction. The boys laugh about other stuff, just like old friends. I am fascinated with this give and take, and any resolution or lack of it. Now, they are busy talking and laughing about other things, especially about people at their old high school.

"Remember when we had the fire drill?" Kenny asks Nathan. "We always went to the top of the steep hill. After the drill, my friend, who is big, ran down the hill really fast and out of control to the parking lot full of cars. He couldn't stop and he jumped over a bumper to barely squeeze past a girl and the car. We laughed for days afterward."

And the boys laughed again in the van and it tickled me.

Kenny had another story. "When I was in Spain, my roommate and I were in a restaurant. Six people were at the table and everyone was talking except him. Then out of nowhere he said, 'So who in here likes Angus Barnes cheese?' It was the funniest thing, so random and it had nothing to do with anything anyone was talking about."

Pretty soon, all three of us were laughing.

It's evening, as we continue to the capital city of Indianapolis. The polis in Indianapolis means 'city' in Greek. It is a city of very tall skyscrapers amidst surrounding tracts of flat land. A juxtaposition for our sense of sight. Or maybe it's a logical geometric configuration – a horizontal line makes an upward right angle of rectangles and another right angle to connect again to the flat horizontal line.

We reach the capitol. Several limestone rectangles connect, almost at random, to support a green dome. Kenny waits in the van while Nathan and I walk to the entrance. It's open, even though it is nearly 9pm, and we go in. But the security guard says they are closed. We ask and he lets us use the bathrooms anyway and we have a look around. We find the rotunda and are struck with the beauty of the white marble columns. They surround the open area on every floor level and count up into the dozens. A grand staircase invites us to climb, but we resist. Light is barely coming through the glass around and above us, but it lights our way to the exit and we join Kenny in the van.

We give the State of Indiana hardly a thought as we head south on I-65 and then we cross the border into Kentucky.

# CHAPTER 20

# KENTUCKY TO NORTH CAROLINA

It's my turn at the wheel. I skirt Louisville, Kentucky, head east and stop just short of Frankfort. This is far enough. It's 11:30 at night and a Best Western motel is shining its lights to welcome us.

I sleep little. My mind is in gyro mode with the dramas of the day and our nearing the end of our trip. We check out of the motel early the next morning, and are on our way. This is our last day on the road.

There is a rainstorm threatening from the west as I merge onto the highway. In spite of the weather, and our sense of urgency, I had every intention of stopping in Frankfort to see the Kentucky state capitol, but somehow I miss the exit. Should I try to turn around on the busy interstate highway, I wonder? Nathan wants to see it but he is too tired to put up an argument and I decide to skip it and press on. I apologize to Nathan. He says he'll see it another time, but I know he's not happy with my decision.

So Indianapolis, Indiana was the last capitol we saw on our trip. And what a full trip it's been. We made time for state capitols and new states, Presidents, history, culture, geography, geology and a lot more. We'll pass up West Virginia's capitol in Charleston, with its newly gilded gold dome. Nathan was there with his brother years ago. Virginia's capitol in Richmond, with no dome at all, is too far to the east. The three of us have seen North Carolina's copper-domed capitol, in Raleigh, dozens of times. I've even met Democratic Governor Mike Easley in the halls.

From Lexington, Kentucky, we have just 440 miles and seven hours to go, to reach North Carolina. Ahead of us are Morehead and Ashland, Kentucky, Huntington and Charleston, West Virginia and Blanch and Wytheville, Virginia. We will pass by Mount Airy, Winston-Salem and Greensboro, North Carolina, and then land home.

Nathan is trying to read from his book The Emperor of Japan: Meiji and His World and doesn't like our interruptions. Kenny, now at the wheel, has wanted to make sure he's making the right turns around Lexington and I want Nathan's confirmation. We sort of know the route but we like the map guy to give his approval. Eventually, we stop asking, and settle into silence and our own thoughts.

The sight of the blue hills of Kentucky, restore us. It is sunny with a cloudless sky. The storm is behind us and I don't think it will catch up. I'm in a tranquil state of mind.

I look at the boys, sitting in front of me, and marvel. They are so young, so new to life, so open to the world. They exude primal energy and élan. They are un-imitated, un-copied and unwonted. And for their short time on earth, they are so wise. The fires of experience have heated, liquefied and molded them. They are stronger for the besiege. The scars and scorn for Nathan, of the cruel teasing he endured in his early years, has given him power. Both boys have weathered isolation in their past. They show boldness, daring and bravery, as the Indians and pioneers did in settling this land. And as the soldiers did, who helped make this country free, and the statesman who figured out how to govern a new unfettered land.

I am proud of these young men. I was pleased with their invitation, and honored that they sincerely wanted me on their travels, that I am moved to silent tears of wonder and gratitude. To share the journey that they are on has made me richer and happier. I'm a better person, knowing their travails and delights.

The rich green Allegheny Mountains of West Virginia, part of the Appalachian chain, surround us now. As we pass over Charleston, we can see the shiny gold dome of the capitol from I-64. Nathan is driving us joyously up and around the slow curves, and is singing forcefully a tune without words. It's not a song we know, but both Kenny and I join in to make a trio of musical sounds. Let the world hear us if it will. We are proclaiming and reclaiming our freedom, our joy and our love of life.

We cross into Virginia and are now passing through the Blue Ridge Mountains, part of the Appalachian chain. Virginia is the birthplace of our nation's independence. The final battle with the British was fought here at Yorktown. Virginia's most famous resident, Thomas Jefferson, is the author of the Declaration of Independence. "Resolved: That these united Colonies are, and of right ought to be free and independent States..."

Across another state border we go. The Blue, Black and, in

Nathan's parlance, the Okee DoeKee Smoky Mountain Ranges of North Carolina are to the west. At Winston-Salem, he makes a swoop to the east. Our trip is nearly over.

It is late afternoon and the light is still strong when we pull up to Nathan's house. It's great to be home, but there is still some accounting to do. Nathan calculates that we each owe $350 for our share of gas and motels, and has figured out how much each of us owes to whom. After some discussion, to my relief, we agree and pay up, and are fair and square. We give final hugs all around.

But, there is still more accounting to do. Before the trip, Nathan had been to 30 states. During the trip he added on 7. And as of my writing, he has been to a total of 44. Before the trip he had been to the Canadian Provinces of Quebec and Ontario. During the trip he added on Manitoba.

Kenny was in 17 states before the trip and, by the end, added 14 states for a total of 31. His total since the trip is 39. Manitoba and Ontario were first time visits for Kenny to Canada.

I, Ethel, added on Kansas, Wyoming and Montana to 41 previously visited states for a total of 44. I had visited Manitoba, Ontario and Quebec in past years.

To see all of the United States, Nathan still has 6 states to go and Kenny has 11.

I, with a lot more years on earth and probably less earth-time left, have only 6 states to go. I start mapping out future journeys in my head.

By the end of the trip, Nathan had been inside the U.S. Capitol and a total of 21 state capitol buildings. Kenny and I haven't figured it out.

In the past few years since the trip, Nathan has been inside the New Mexico capitol at Santa Fe, and the Colorado capitol at Denver, did get to go inside the Kentucky capitol at Frankfort, and managed to return to Winnipeg with a college friend, where he took a full tour of the Manitoba Legislative Building and saw the Elm Trees in all their August splendor.

"Guys," I murmur, with a catch in my voice. "This trip with you has been incredibly rich for me." I pause just long enough for Nathan to inject, "Did you pick up gold in the Dakotas, without our knowing it?"

"No!" I laugh. "But what I have is worth more. My time with you, on our travels, has been a treasure full of joy and learning. You have taught me to love more and appreciate more. You are incredible creations of the Universe. Thank you both for the gift of this trip, and for being who you are. I wish you each an Aristotle dose of happiness on your life's adventure. He says 'to flourish' is the highest good. Keep flourishing, dear boys!"

"We will," they both say with smiles, "and thank you for coming with us."

I hug each of the boys and they hug me back warmly. Home is beckoning, and the Hobbit in me returns gratefully to my small cottage in the woods. My life is reverberating with the extraordinary times I shared with two uncommon boys. The good fortune to know them is mine.

# AFTERWORD

A week after our trip ended, Nathan and a friend made a trip to the Appalachian Mountains and climbed to the top of Mount Mitchell in North Carolina, 6,684 feet or 2,037 meters, the highest point in the eastern half of North America. They climbed 12 miles and got lost for 6 more miles. Two months later Kenny joined them on a second trip to Mt. Mitchell. Like the bears in Canada, sharing the same climate at this North Carolina altitude, they ate raspberries, blackberries and blueberries. They drank crystal clear spring water from the source, and as Nathan reported, "they even had a cloud float up the mountain, swallow them up and rain upon them before tumbling down the eastern side."

After our trip, Kenny started playing poker about 25 hours per week and makes enough to pay for food and an occasional trip. Along with the poker, he sporadically takes online classes, sometimes passing and sometimes not. He would still be at a freshman level at college, even if he were so inclined. He still lives at home, sees friends, plays board games and goes to an occasional party. He is not hunting for a job, but he is looking for a girlfriend.

Nathan has completed his college degree, Summa Cum Laude, with a major in East Asian Languages and Cultures, with Concentrations in Japanese and Chinese, and minors in both Russian Studies and Physics. He speaks seven languages conversationally, including Arabic. He has received many honors including membership in Phi Beta Kappa.

He worked throughout his college years in a work-study program, tutoring Japanese and Russian, cleaning up in the college cafes and doing grounds keeping.

He is now attending law school. He wants to use his many languages in the world of international business law.

The Whitehall Depot, in my hometown, was placed on the National Register of Historic Places in 2006. Photos of my father, Depot Agent and Telegrapher Arvid B Erickson, will soon be on display, along with papers that he kept. He deserves his place in history.

I, Ethel, as writer of our story, get the last word. I stay in close touch with both Nathan and Kenny, on the phone or in person. They talk, we laugh, they ask for my ideas about things, we see movies. They show an interest in my life and I in theirs. I continue to travel, make music and write.